POSTCARDS

from

HEAVEN

Messages of Love from the Other Side

DAN GORDON

FREE PRESS

New York London Toronto Sydney

FREE PRESS
A Division of Simon & Schuster, Inc.
1230 Avenue of the Americas
New York, NY 10020

First Free Press hardcover edition November 2008

FREE PRESS and colophon are trademarks of Simon & Schuster, Inc.

For information about special discounts for bulk purchases,
please contact Simon & Schuster Special Sales at 1-800-456-6798
or business@simonandschuster.com

Book design by Ellen R. Sasahara

Manufactured in the United States of America

1   3   5   7   9   10   8   6   4   2

Library of Congress Cataloging-in-Publication Data

Gordon, Dan.

Postcards from heaven: messages of love from the other side /
by Dan Gordon.

p. cm.

1. Spiritualism 2. Gordon, Dan. I. Title.
BF1301.G765 2008
133.901'3—dc22
2008002210

ISBN-13: 978-1-4165-8829-0
ISBN-10:   1-4165-8829-9

For Zaki

{ Contents }

{ FOREWORD }

Dan Gordon is a master storyteller, and in his profound book he has shared his personal family stories. They are real; they come from the heart, and they inspire us all to take a glimpse into our own lives and ponder the possibilities of life after death. Dan's simple book of life is much more complex than it appears. It encourages us to ask profound and powerful questions about our own lives.

We all have a story. Our stories differ according to our personal circumstances, but still they belong to us. In my own journey, I try to make sense of the complexity of life. I want to believe that life is eternal. I have no concrete proof of that but I know that, when I think about it, it changes the way I feel about everything. What a different world it would be if we could look at life and death differently. If life were indeed eternal, how would we all go about our lives? Would we worry about death; about getting old; about money, jobs, relationships? Wouldn't we simply focus on being alive and fully functioning on this planet . . . right now? Would we say I love you . . . and mean it? Would we cease to care what others thought? Would we begin appreciating the small things that life is offering? I believe that our world would begin to expand. We would see—and more importantly, we would feel—the shift taking place within.

When my father passed away, I was filled with sadness, from worrying about my mother and how she would manage without him.

How could she continue to live alone in the home they had shared for sixty-two years?

One afternoon after his memorial I walked into a large commercial store, and they were playing my father's favorite song over the loudspeaker, Louis Armstrong's "What a Wonderful World." I stopped and immediately knew, and felt, that this was my postcard, my own personal postcard from Heaven. The thought that "Dad" was there with me through this song was enough to change my feelings from sadness to appreciation. My vibration had changed. Did I miss him? You bet. Did I want to be able to sit down and talk with him in this noisy building? Yep! I wandered aimlessly around the store, pushing my cart, fully listening to every word of the song, and I felt my feelings go from sadness to appreciation. Appreciation for the time we did have together on this planet: appreciation for him being my father; for giving me values that I adhere to to this day; and for so many, many valuable lessons.

Do we have the answers to life and death? Probably not, but this wonderful book opens us up to the grand notion that perhaps life just might be eternal . . . the ultimate postcard.

With great love and respect I encourage you to read Dan's stories with an open mind and heart and explore your own life stories—and watch the postcards come flying in.

Linda Gray

I would venture that nearly all of us either have had or have heard of an experience in which a soul already departed reaches back to those of us who have been left behind in this world with a reassuring touch. Sometimes it's no more than a whisper, a familiar smell in the air, or just the feeling of presence as vivid as when the loved one was still alive. These moments are just that . . . moments, a glimpse behind the veil; not a letter from heaven, but a postcard.

There are those who believe that what we call life ends with what they call death. They either do not believe that there is such a thing as a soul, or if there is a soul, that it dies with the body. I think such people are like frightened children—afraid to be disappointed, to be deprived of that which they most desire—so they deny that what they want even exists. They hide their heads beneath a security blanket of science and reason, arguing that no one can empirically prove the existence of the soul eternal and, therefore, it does not exist. Believing in a soul, to them, is little more than superstition.

To me, their argument is like suggesting that various waves of energy, which science can measure, could not possibly have existed before the advent of the instruments with which we measure them. Of course, the opposite is true. Light waves have existed for as long as there has been light, but the spectrometer that measures those waves has been here for less than a century. Indeed, only recently has a theory been offered explaining that light exists both as a particle and a wave at the same time. This seeming contradiction, however, is not within the nature of light but within our ability to define it, to put it in the proper box, to make it conform to the proper rule. While it's true that we humans certainly created the theory of the moment, we most assuredly did not create light. Light is light. Our ability to understand it is evolving, but no matter how we define it, we won't affect its properties or the reality of its existence.

Thus, I believe it is with the soul. The soul is. Only our ability to define and measure the soul is evolving, which brings us to two things: faith and anecdotal evidence. This slim volume attests to both: faith in the existence of life after death and anecdotal evidence—the postcards from heaven, if you will, which illustrate and celebrate that existence.

Their message has comforted me, and I hope it will do the same for you. It is a simple one, really:

Got here safe.
It's really beautiful.
Much much love till we meet again.

{ THE SPACESUIT }

My Sweetheart, who is as wise as she is beautiful, refers to death as taking off the spacesuit.

Imagine you were an astronaut, out for a little space walk, puttering around the station perhaps, fixing up the solar panels, when suddenly you encountered a being from another galaxy. Let us say that you and the being exchanged astronaut pleasantries and looked each other over, possibly even touched each other, and then your new E.T. friend vanished, headed back to the mother ship all atwitter with news of the strange new species he had just encountered.

That being from a galaxy far far away would probably describe you as looking like their equivalent of the Pillsbury Doughboy or the Michelin Man. You were, he would report, bulky and white, with a glassy countenance. Then he might suggest that he believed that the spacesuit was just an outer shell. Underneath it, he believed, he had glimpsed something wonderful, graceful, elastic, muscular, and so much more beautiful than its bulky carapace.

I can imagine his cynical alien boss pooh-poohing the notion. "I've seen them," he might say. "And what you see is what you get. There is no inner earthling, separate and alive, which animates the outer earthling. Why," he might add, "I have even had occasion to measure their life span. It is there in the rectangular hump on their backs. It is called oxygen and when it runs out they die. Period. End of story."

So it is with us, says my Sweetheart. What some call Death is simply a discarding of the spacesuit. That's what we bury, the old suit, no longer needed.

I was there when my brother got a glimpse of that place where spacesuits are no longer necessary. I was there when he took off his suit, and later . . . when he sent me a postcard from the other side.

{ DAVID }

My brother David and I did not have an easy relationship with our father. It was through no fault of my dad's, stemming rather, I believe, from the fact that he was born in 1895 in Czarist Russia, in a village that had neither electricity nor running water. He came from thirteen generations of Hassidic rabbis who demanded and received unquestioning obedience: The "Papa" was always right. That his children would question any of his edicts was unthinkable to my father.

To complicate matters, my father was an orphan by the time he was eleven, so perhaps even the memory of how a father related to his children was too dim and distant by the time we appeared. Add to that the fact that my dad had married and had children later in life than was the norm, and you had the recipe for intergenerational trench warfare.

My dad was born into nineteenth-century feudalism and we were born into rock 'n' roll.

The result, predictably, was disaster.

Everything we did—the way we walked, talked, the way we sat slouched, one leg draped across the armrest of the sofa—drove him crazy. Most of all, the way in which we questioned his authority was to him, the height of disrespect.

For us, everything he did in reaction to our Americanisms seemed nuts. As a result, my brother David, six years older than I, left the house by the time he was seventeen. Six years later, I left home at the age of sixteen in an agreed-upon separation.

Having seen the motion picture *Exodus,* and having been smitten by the character of Jordana Ben Canaan and her rather fetching short shorts, I wanted to go to live on a kibbutz in Israel, assuming that the real-life counterpart of the fictional Ms. Ben Canaan was to be found somewhere on a collective in the Valley of Jezreel. My parents were relieved to let me go.

In high school there, I fell in love with a number of Jordana Ben Canaan surrogates, as well as the kibbutz lifestyle, but came back to the States to go to college, studying filmmaking at UCLA. Through a fluke, I wound up selling my first screenplay to Universal Studios when I was twenty years old. Later, I moved back to Israel and lived there for most of the 1970s, returning to the United States in 1980. Thereafter, I enjoyed a successful career as a screenwriter, based in Los Angeles. My brother David, despite my father's predictions to the contrary, became a successful real estate developer and made his first million by the time he was thirty.

Papa took pride in our accomplishments and both of us respected him—respected his honesty and his ironclad work ethic which meant that his word was his bond. There was at least a general cessation of hostilities between generations. But it would not be until much later that David and Papa would finally be at peace with each other. My big brother was six years older than me and I not only loved him, I idolized him.

When he was forty-three, he was diagnosed with a brain tumor and given three months to live.

Shortly before David was diagnosed he was faced with what, for some men, would have been a difficult decision. Both his wife's and daughter's birthdays were October eleventh and he had been planning an elaborate celebration for the double birthdays. But as the day for the big event neared, he was offered a chance to go moose hunting in Alaska. In his defense, it was not just the chance to go moose hunting but the chance to go moose hunting with a legendary guide who was usually booked up three years or more in advance. A friend had booked the guide, but someone had fallen out of the party and a space was available. As I say, for some men that would have been a difficult decision, but not for my brother. He reasoned that birthdays come every year but the opportunity to go after moose in Alaska with a legendary guide does not. So, while less decisive men would have faltered, my brother immediately sent in his deposit and booked his flight to Anchorage. In what he thought was a splendid gesture of magnanimity, he announced that he would delay the birthday party but was dedicating the hunt to his wife and daughter.

The hunt was eventful. David was on horseback when he spotted a giant bull moose that turned out to be of almost record proportions. He swung out of his saddle, pulled his .30-06 out of its scabbard, and, just then, the wind shifted. The moose smelled my brother and charged. David was shaking so badly that he missed the first shot clean.

The moose kept charging.

The second shot did no better.

The moose was now within thirty meters and closing fast.

David squeezed off what he knew would be his last round, as there would be no time for a fourth shot. He hit the moose square in the chest, but the momentum of the charge continued to propel the giant beast forward, toward my brother.

He came to rest, finally, only a few feet from David, whereupon the hunting guide proclaimed, "I'll tell you what. For a while there I didn't know if we wuz gonna have us a picture of a Jew with his foot on the moose, or a picture of a moose with his foot on the Jew."

David told that story at the party he arranged for his wife and daughter not long after. After the punchline, he collapsed in a full grand mal seizure and began break dancing on the floor.

The diagnosis was cancer. A glioblastoma multiforme to be precise, pressing on David's brain. He underwent surgery that night, which was successful in that they were able to remove most of the tumor. But this particular tumor was of such a virulent nature that it would have grown back on the brain stem even if the doctor had removed all of it and David's brain as well. The doctor told my brother that he was fortunate to have three months to live, which would allow him to put his affairs in order before he died. Whatever karma my brother might have incurred through the death of the moose was about to be paid off with interest.

David actually battled the disease for a year and a half, undergoing several terrifying, torturous experimental procedures that would have done Dr. Frankenstein proud.

I had traveled with David and his wife, Linda, to see a renowned doctor who was working on a new protocol that seemed to hold some promise in treating tumors like my brother's. The doctor explained that there were actually two protocols and my brother was free to choose whichever one he wished to be a part of. The first involved taking a drug orally, which would make the tumor more vulnerable to radiation treatments that would be localized and focused into the center of the malignancy. There were relatively few side effects other than those normally associated with radiation.

The second protocol involved bolting a metal halo to the patient's skull. Once the halo was in place, it was used to clamp the patient to the operating table so that a hole could be bored into the skull itself. Because they had to know if they were touching any inappropriate areas of the brain, the patient was required to be awake during the entire procedure. Then a radioactive isotope was to be placed into the center of the tumor and left there for several weeks. The patient would be required to wear a steel helmet, not to protect himself, mind you, but to protect the doctors, nurses, and visitors within a six-foot radius of the radiation emanating from the patient's skull.

Both protocols seemed to have similar cure rates. Which would my brother like to choose?

"I don't know," said David. "I got an idea—why don't we just open up a hole in the roof and fly a kite out of it on a length of copper wire and tie the other end of the wire around my head and wait for lightning to strike! I mean that sounds about the same, right?"

I thought that was pretty funny.

The doctor did not.

"All right," David said, seeing that the doctor was taking this entirely too seriously. "Lemme think . . . hmm . . . take a pill or drill a hole into my skull and plant a radioactive isotope in my brain . . . hmm . . . what to choose, what to choose . . . hmm . . . okay . . . got it! Call me cuckoo but I'll choose the pill."

"This is a serious decision," said the doctor. "I don't think this is something you want to joke about."

"Oh, no joke," David said. "I want the pill instead of the radioactive isotope drilled into my head."

"Well," said the doctor, clearly disappointed, "you have plenty of time to choose. Both protocols require a six-week dose of chemotherapy beforehand. So you can just go back to Los Angeles and your oncologist there will handle the chemo and then when it's done you can come back and make your decision."

Fair enough. So that's what we did. David underwent six weeks of chemo and all the joys associated with that.

Then we traveled back to see the doctor, whereupon David told the good doctor that he would still opt for what was behind door number one: namely, the pill, as opposed to the hole being drilled into his skull and filled with Day-Glo.

The doctor looked nonplussed and said, "Gee . . ."

"Gee . . . what?"

"Well if that's what you wanted," said the doctor, "you really should have let me know beforehand. That protocol was closed two weeks ago. I'm afraid it's all filled up."

"But . . ." said my brother, whose speech was hesitant by now and noticeably slurred because of the pressure of the tumor pressing against his brain, "you said . . . I had the time . . . the time, you know . . . you said . . ."

David looked over at me. I had by then begun to translate for him when he couldn't find the word he wanted to say.

I nodded my head and said to the doctor, "You said David had to have six weeks of chemotherapy for either protocol and that he could take that time to decide."

David nodded his head up and down and said, "Yes!" forcefully.

"Mr. Gordon," the doctor said to me, as if my brother weren't in the room, "your brother, of course, has a brain tumor. He may have thought that's what I said. Auditory confusion is to be expected."

"Not confused!" David said, shaking his head back and forth.

"He's not confused," I said, "and neither am I. And I don't have a brain tumor. You said he had six weeks to decide."

"That's exactly what he said," Linda said, putting her hand on David's shoulder protectively.

"Well," said the doctor, "if I did, then I misspoke."

"No harm, no foul. Just put him on the first protocol, the one with the pill, and everything will be fine."

"As I said, that protocol is full. It's closed. Your brother will go on the second protocol."

"You told him he had six weeks to decide."

"Well, now I'm telling him something else."

I inherited a very bad temper from my father. So did my brother. I could feel his anger as well as my own beginning to swell and blacken the room. I tried to not let the monster I had seen so often in my father get loose.

I said, "That's a very cavalier attitude, don't you think, Doctor?"

I knew that I had a certain look on my face. It was not a look that came from my father. When my Dad was about to lose it, he looked nuts, his muscles would twitch, and he would shake with an anger that would take over his body. That wasn't the look I felt on my face. This look was different.

The first movie of mine that got made, but was never distributed, I wrote for some mafia guys who, it turned out later, ran a money-laundering operation, though I didn't know it at the time. Those guys loved me. They called me The Orange because I came from California and was so naïve that, upon seeing the baseball bats they all carried in their cars and had in their offices, I had actually asked them if they sponsored a Little League team.

They loved that.

I was fresh out of college. It was 1972, during the Columbo / Gallo war. They were not associated with either of those families, but still they knew that Crazy Joey Gallo might be tempted to strike out against them to send them a message to stay out of things. As the gentleman they called Johnny Spic said to me, "What's he gonna do? Hit one of us? He hits one of us an' I got a hundred button men in the street tomorra' comin' after him. So he's not gonna hit one of us. He's gonna hit an investment. You're an investment. I want ya's protected." Whereupon he introduced me to my bodyguard, Muff the Button Man.

Muff the Button Man lived with me for nine months. He was six four, weighed about three hundred pounds, and always had a .38 and a .45 on him as well as a little two-shot derringer he kept in something that looked like a billfold. He called it a wallet gun.

"Muff," I said, after we had roomed together for almost a year, "you're a button man, right?"

"Yeah," said Muff.

"And that means . . ."

"Dat means if Johnny Spic wants to push da button on somebody . . . I push da button."

"Right," I said. "Now you and I have become friends, right?"

"Friends?" said Muff, genuinely hurt. "We're brothers." Though when he said it, it came out "Bruvers."

"Right," I said. "We're bruvers . . . but . . . if Johnny Spic told you to push the button on me . . . you'd do it, right?"

"Jeez," he said. "You know how to pose what you wanna call your moral dilemma. I tell ya's what. If I had anything to say about it . . . I mean anything what-so-fu#*ing-ever . . . you wouldn't feel a thing."

That was the best deal my friend Muff could cut me.

So when I looked at the doctor it was not the kind of look that my father used to wear when he got angry. It was the kind of look I'd seen on Johnny Spic when he told Muff the Button Man to push the button.

The doctor had probably never been around anyone like Johnny Spic so he misread the look.

"That's a very cavalier attitude, don't you think, Doctor?" I repeated, looking at him like Johnny Spic making a business decision.

"Who do you think you're looking at like that?" said the doctor. Then he leaned in toward me and spoke as if our discussion were just between the two of us, "You're beginning to antagonize me. And when you come to think about it, I have your brother's life in my hands. I'm probably the last person you want to antagonize . . . aren't I?"

"Oh, Doctor," I said, completely losing the look, "if that's the impression I gave you, I just want to apologize. We go on whatever protocol you think best."

"But he said . . ." David's wife protested.

"The doctor knows what he's doing," I said. "Why don't you guys wait outside a minute and let me get the details from the doctor. I'm so sorry, Doctor," I said.

Once they were outside, I wrote a phone number on a piece of paper and said, "What do you know about me, Doctor?"

"You're some sort of movie writer," he said in what I can only call a dismissive tone.

"That's right," I said. "A rich movie writer. And the first movie I wrote was for some guys in the Genovese family. They love me. Go figure, huh? Now, this is a phone number of a gentleman in New Jersey. I want you to call that number to verify what I'm saying. I'm a rich man, Doctor, made a lot of money."

"If you think you can influence this hospital or my superiors by making some sort of donation, I'll have you know that I'm not only a tenured professor but the head of this department. Now get out of here and—"

"Oh, I'm gonna make a donation, Doctor. Trust me. Either my brother's on that protocol or I'm going to make a donation to Muff the Button Man and have you killed. I'll put twenty-five grand on the street as soon as I leave here and it'll look like two junkies murdered you for your wallet in the park."

This time he got it.

"Clerical error," I said when I joined my brother in the hall. "You're on the protocol after all."

"You threaten to kill him?" David asked.

"You bet."

The protocol did not work.

It slowed the growth of the tumor for a while. But then it came back harder than ever.

That's when David decided to try the other protocol—the Frankenstein treatment—where they drilled the hole and planted Chernobyl in your brain. He did it not so much because he thought it could cure him, though he hoped there was a shot at that. He did it mainly because he believed that, regardless of what happened to him, the doctors would learn from it, and someone down the line would benefit, even if he didn't.

It wasn't *The Passion of the Christ* to be sure, but it wasn't a flu shot, either. There was the business of the halo. It was David's own crown of thorns, though in this case it was a metal band screwed into his skull with spokes that radiated out to the halo. Once they'd put the halo in place, they told David that he'd have about a forty-five-minute wait until the skull drilling began. David said that he had to go to the john, so we went off in search of a restroom, which we were told was just down the hall. Even with the halo bolted in place David could walk with me supporting him. He had already begun milking the tumor thing, as in, "Don't blame me for the faux pas, I've got a brain tumor." The halo gave him additional immunity from prosecution. Thus, armed with an excuse for any behavior no matter how outrageous, we started down the hall toward the promised bathroom.

David was a terrifying sight, truly Frankenstein-like, with dried blood on his forehead near where the halo was bolted in. A few steps into our stroll we heard a twelve-year-old crying as he was being prepped for surgery.

David poked his head into the kid's room and the poor tyke gasped at my brother in horror.

"Hey, kid," my brother said with his sort of slurry speech and a whacked-out look in his eye and the bolts in his skull. "What are you in for?"

"They . . . they're gonna take my tonsils out," said the terrified kid.

"Oh yeah?" said my brother, "Me too."

I can still hear the kid's scream.

My brother had an impish sense of humor.

Once back in the operating room, David had a sheet pulled up to his neck as they clamped the halo to a frame to immobilize his head. Before they began the surgery the doctor once again explained that, since they were going into very sensitive areas of the brain, David would have to be awake for the entire procedure. It was imperative, the doctor said, that David tell them immediately if he felt anything unusual.

"Unusual?" They were about to drill into his skull! Well, there would be local anesthetic for that but they needed David to tell them once they were in there if he felt anything strange, or painful, or otherwise. They were going to be in an area of the brain where if they touched the wrong thing, they could leave him paralyzed, speechless, or blind.

David heard the whirring sound as they drilled and then they got ready to implant the isotope. That's when David said, "I feel something."

The doctors all jumped back lest they further damage what was left of my brother's brain.

"Can you describe the feeling?" the doctor asked.

"Yessss . . ." said my brother tentatively. "It's somewhat tingly. . . ."

"Yes?" said the doctor, leaning toward him.

"And not altogether unpleasant," David said, and as he said it he raised his fingers beneath the sheet to the twelve o'clock position, as if he were getting an erection.

The nurse broke up laughing. So did one of the surgeons.

The head surgeon, however, was not amused.

"We are doing brain surgery here!" he said, "Brain surgery! And you make a joke like that! You are without a doubt one of the biggest a@#holes I have ever met in my life!"

"Well, Doctor," my brother said with what I had begun to think of as a charming slur, "you all looked so serious. I just thought, if I'm not nervous, why should you be?"

I've seen brave men in my life. None like that.

Every morning, David's stepson Jeff and I would stop off at a renowned local café and pick up an order of their corned beef hash to go. My brother was partial to that. We'd smuggle it in to him. Then we'd bring in videotapes of Mel Brooks movies and John Belushi routines. We had to wear metal aprons to protect us from the radiation even though he wore his steel helmet, so I'd bring in packets of microwave popcorn and as a joke hold them up to his head. We had our popcorn and comedy festival and I expect we never laughed so much in our lives. Except for the fact that he was dying, we had a great time.

In the final six months, as the tumor grew, my brother would undergo the trials of Job, gradually losing the ability to walk, see, and, finally, speak.

His mind, however, stayed intact, imprisoned in a body, once so graceful and athletic, that had all but ceased to function.

Two days before he died, he slipped into a coma. As he did so, he smiled. It was the most beautiful smile I have ever seen.

I don't know what he saw as he slipped over to the other side. I know only what he said. "It's so beautiful," he whispered. "So beautiful."

But he did not die; he woke up a day and a half later.

His eyes opened suddenly. He looked around the room and then spoke as clear as a bell (though for the last month he had all but lost the ability to speak). "F@*k," he said. "I'm back!"

He was not happy.

Thankfully, later that day he went back into a coma. I sat next to him almost the whole time. And as I sat there I reflected on the fact that, as my big brother, David had always gone first and eased the way for me. I would never have gotten away with near as much had David not done everything bad first.

It was New Year's Eve when he passed. Just before his soul departed, whatever he had seen earlier he must have seen again. For that smile appeared once more.

After that, it was just a spacesuit he no longer needed.

I now believe that as always in our lives, my brother had gone across first to check things out and then had come back to reassure us that the place he was about to enter was so very beautiful, and that as delightful as our company no doubt was, nothing on this earth could compare with what awaited us in the place he had just visited. As with the Alaskan hunt, he just had to come back to tell us the story.

I have felt my brother's presence many times since then. Not as a presence nearby. Not next to me. But inside me. Sometimes I see his expression looking back at me in the mirror, or in the odd photograph; a delicious ironic look full of mischief. I know the way I look, the full range of expressions, and I promise you that one's not mine, nor is it Johnny Spic's, nor is it Muff the Button Man's. It is my brother David peeking out through my eyes, sharing a smile or a laugh at a joke that no one but the two of us would ever understand. It is a postcard.

{ PAPA }

My father died less than three months after my brother.

He was an old man and there was no sadness in his death. Truth is, he could have done without the last year and a half of his life, without seeing his firstborn son die before him.

My father lived to be ninety-one. He had lived a full life that took him through the First World War, the Russian Revolution, and the civil war that followed it. My dad had broken with his family's legacy. He came from thirteen generations of Hassidic rabbis, some of them very famous. His grandfather, my great-grandfather, Rabbi Yisrael Ben Shmuel Dov, was chief justice of the Rabbinical Court in his province. A pious man, he was known far and wide for rendering all his decisions flawlessly from memory, having had to memorize all the tracts upon which rabbinical law is based because he was blind. He became known as Der Blinder Rebbe, the Blind Rabbi.

When he was in his eighties, my great-grandfather decided that it was time to realize his dream and go to die in the Holy Land. His congregants paid his passage and that of the young rabbi who was to accompany him. So he went up to dwell in Jerusalem, to die in the City of David.

But, as luck would have it, things did not work out the way he had planned. Instead of dying, he lived to be 104 years old. I've heard differing numbers, some as high as 112, but all of them were well over a hundred. He became a famous rabbi in Jerusalem and, when he died, was front-page news in the first Hebrew newspaper of the day, *Havatselet*. He was buried in a spot reserved for holy men called The Portion of the Righteous on the Mount of Olives with a front-row seat for the coming of the Messiah.

You can imagine what my father's ancestors must have felt when my father became a cowboy.

Papa, as my sons called him, and as I came to think of him, was born near Poltava, Russia. When he was eleven, his father, who was also, of course, a rabbi, was in another village when suddenly the photograph of him hanging on the wall fell. Thereupon my grandmother let out a cry and announced that her husband was dead. Her children tried to console her and tell her that she had no way of knowing such a thing, but she would not be consoled. It turned out that her husband had indeed died, as near as anyone could later tell, right around the time the photograph fell off the wall seemingly of its own accord.

My father's family was very superstitious, but then perhaps they had reason to be.

At an early age my father announced to his father that when he grew up he was going to be a Zionist and emigrate to Israel. Zionism, the political movement to rebuild the land of Israel, was close to heresy in my grandfather's house. Redeeming Israel could be accomplished only by the Messiah, and speaking Hebrew, the holy language, as an everyday means of communication was believed to be blasphemy. But my father was steadfast in his determination to do both. In the last days of World War I, when the Russian Revolution and later the Bolshevik Revolution and the civil war swept through the Ukraine, the area around Poltava bounced back and forth between nations and political movements like a ping-pong ball. One week it was Russians, then Germans, then Poles, then Ukrainian nationalists, then Red Russians, and then White. Each time someone new came over they had themselves a little pogrom.

Killing Jews always seemed to give the locals and their latest occupiers something they could agree on.

The young Zionist boys decided to fight back. They were already organized but now needed arms. So, in his early twenties, my father became a train robber with his pals, stealing a load of arms off a Czech train. They then formed up into platoons and undertook the defense of the Jewish community in and around Poltava. (Sixty years later I was serving in a reserve armored infantry unit in the Israeli army. Of the eight guys with whom I shared an armored personnel carrier, four of them had fathers who had come from Poltava. Not only had they all come from the same town but all had married late in life and were now in their seventies and eighties. Not only were they close to the same age, but all of them had served together in the Zionist self-defense units in which my father had served, in Poltava, during the Russian civil war. They all knew one another. They all remembered one another, and now their sons were serving not only in the same army but the same vehicle! So maybe my father had a right to be superstitious.)

After the Communists won the war, anyone who had served in a rival faction's military or paramilitary organization had a death sentence on his head. Papa got word that he was to be arrested and left his home that night, making his way to Warsaw, where he lived for a year. Hooking up with a Zionist group there that was going to go to Israel to found a kibbutz in the Galilee, he made it as far as Milano, Italy, where he was arrested for not having any travel documents. He was thrown into jail and was set to be deported to Russia, which for him would have been a death sentence.

Now, Papa was the baby in his family. He had a much older brother, my uncle Hyman, whom he really didn't know that well but who had come out to Canada years before. Uncle Hyman originally wanted to settle in Montreal but he was told politely but firmly that they had all the Jews they could use in Montreal. However, the

Canadian government was interested in immigrants going to Alberta province, which was at the time inhabited mainly by Blackfoot Indians, or, as Uncle Hyman called them, Schvartze Fisselach.

So Uncle Hyman went west and became a cattle rancher, and a wealthy one at that. He owned cattle, bred racehorses, and was an inveterate gambler who liked to race his convertible against trains to the railroad crossing. He lost to the train once, but not even a train could kill my uncle, who was a very tough old bird.

So my father, in jail in Milano, wired his wealthy brother in Canada for help, and Uncle Hyman came through, sending over a thousand dollars to my father, enough to bribe his way out of the Italian jail, enough to falsify documents and buy steam ship tickets, and enough to get Papa all the way to Lethbridge, Alberta, Canada.

When he got there, my dad told his brother that he would always be in his debt and that there was no way he could ever repay him.

Uncle Hyman said that brought up an interesting point: how *did* my dad intend to repay him?

Well, my father said, he would get a job.

Who would hire him? Uncle Hyman asked. My father couldn't speak English. He was a complete greenhorn. No. It was already decided. My father would work for my uncle on one of Uncle Hyman's ranches, I think at Pincher Creek. At any rate, that's how Papa became a cowboy.

The truth is, that is pretty much the story of the Canadian West. It wasn't guys who looked like John Wayne or Gary Cooper who tamed the land. It was guys who looked like my dad—a Russian Jewish Yiddish-speaking cowpoke—and other guys with accents: Scotsmen and Poles and Ukrainians and Jews.

When I was a kid we used to go up most summers to one of Uncle Hyman's ranches. Among other things, he supplied bucking stock to the Calgary Stampede, so my brother David and I got to see the rodeo from the chutes. It was every little boy's dream. We had our own ponies for the summer and slept in the bunkhouse or in an attic bedroom above the kitchen where Aunt Mary would be up at four thirty in the morning, making enormous breakfasts for the ranch hands: steak, eggs, strawberries in fresh cream. Now and then in the evening, one of the hands, or my uncle, would let my brother and me have sips of beer. Our cousins Manuel and Sam were pilots who flew Piper Cubs and let both my brother and me go up with them. *Flying* Jewish cowboys! It was better than the television series *Sky King*.

One day my uncle woke me up and said, "Danil, you vant to come and see der Indians? This is not like the television, not Tonto or Shmonto. These are the Emes Indians. Kim shein, get up. I've got good friends from the Schvartze Fisselach."

We saddled up and rode out to the reservation, my Uncle Hyman and I and my cousin Morris. This was 1952 or 1953, but it was like a scene out of *Dances with Wolves*. There were tepees and skins drying on racks and kids jumping through cook fires and generally getting into trouble with their mothers. All the Blackfeet, or Schvartze Fisselach (which was what I believed their tribal name to be until I was about ten years old), seemed to know Uncle Hyman. One elderly Indian came out of a tepee to greet us. He had on a flannel shirt and a vest and the Willie Nelson headband and braids. We are talking Chief Dan George here, by the looks of him. My uncle shot him a little sign language and said Nee-wash teh, or something to that effect. Whereupon the old Indian looked at my uncle and me and said, "Vus machs du Hyman? Dos is der kleiner? Oy a schoener bucher!" (Wassup, Hyman? This is the little one? Oh, a cute kid!)

When I saw *Blazing Saddles* I thought it was a documentary. Finally a film that told the truth about the Old West as I knew it.

At any rate, Dad went to work as a ranch hand for my uncle, with a work contract, which had to be paid off. Now, on that ranch there was a *zoftig* little French Canadian woman named Mimi, who was

Papa's main squeeze, a hot little number who had a work contract as a cook. I saw the one surviving picture of them. My dad is sitting in the back of a hay wagon with Mimi in his lap. His right hand is grabbing her ass and they're both smiling.

But one night my father caught her in the backseat of a model A with a cattle buyer (who my cousin Manuel believes was the same Yiddish-speaking Indian I later met). So Papa headed up to the big house, which is what they called the house where Uncle Hyman, Aunt Mary, and their four children lived.

As I said before, Uncle Hyman liked to gamble, and he had what my father said was a rather famous poker game every week at his home. There were ranchers, oilmen, and even a Blackfoot chief who had a good deal of money from mineral rights. It was the height of the Depression and, according to Papa, there was ten thousand dollars on the table. (Papa was earning twenty-six dollars a month at the time, or so he said. It should be remembered that storytelling is an inherited art form in my family. According to Papa, he and his brother had been feuding and, outside of what was necessary to run a ranch, hadn't spoken directly to each other in over a year.)

"I need to speak with you," Papa told his brother in Yiddish.

Uncle Hyman looked at him and said, "Abrash, there's a game going on."

Papa said it was about the French Canadian woman, the cook, Mimi. He wanted her off the ranch and sent packing to Montreal the next day. Any money she owed on her work contract he would pay off.

"That's it?" Uncle Hyman asked.

"That's it."

The next day Mimi was gone. My father never spoke to her again. I found her picture tucked away among his effects after he died. My mother looked at it and said, "That's the Mimi woman." Then she walked away.

Papa continued working on the ranch and played semipro ice hockey for the Lethbridge and Calgary teams in the wintertime, and Canada, not Israel, became his home. He lived frugally, left the ranch, saved his money, and at the age of forty-four decided it was time to take a wife. He asked a friend of his where the best-looking women in North America were.

"No doubt about it," said the friend. "Southern California."

So Papa took his life savings, which amounted to almost three thousand dollars, and headed down from the great Northwest to Southern California to find a bride.

It was 1939. He had a friend in Long Beach who said that there was going to be a mixer of young Jewish singles at the bar of a beach-front hotel. He ought to check it out.

He did.

That's where he met Goddess.

{ MOM }

That was my mother's real name . . . Goddess.

She hated it.

She always blamed it on my aunt Dora.

Whereas my father's family were poor but pious Russian Jewish rabbis, my mother was descended from some of the only Russian Jewish nobility. The Baron Poliakov was knighted by the Czar for having built the Trans-Siberian Railway. He had extensive land holdings and homes in Moscow and St. Petersburg as well as a large estate in the Ukraine.

By 1905 however, Eli Poliakov, one of the old baron's descendants, could see the handwriting of approaching revolution on the wall. He packed up his wife, Rose, and nine children and left for the other Promised Land: America.

By all accounts, like most of the Pollikoffs, as they now called themselves, Eli was a thoroughly charming, bright, and financially inept man.

He bought a farm in Illinois because land to a Russian was equated with wealth and position. Unfortunately, he knew absolutely nothing about farming in Illinois and was forced to sell the place.

He then bought a farm in Missouri and failed at that.

Next came a general store, at which he also failed. He died young, barely fifty, a charming man who had lost an extraordinary amount of money.

My aunt Dora was my mother's eldest sibling. She remembered palatial estates and obedient muzhik serfs. I stayed with her once in her New York apartment when I was sixteen and on my way to Israel and the kibbutz, where I would go to high school (of which Aunt Dora heartily disapproved). I came in to breakfast in a pair of shorts and a T-shirt. But that is not why she shrieked. She shrieked because of my feet.

"Your feet!" she shrieked, pointing at them.

I looked at my feet.

They looked okay to me.

"What's wrong with them, Aunt Dora?" I asked.

"They are bare!" she said in her perfect Russian (not Yiddish) accent. She pointed imperiously at my offending bare feet.

"So what?" I asked.

"So vat?" she exclaimed like the dowager empress. "Young man, do you know that ven I arise I step from my bed into my slippers, from my slippers into my stockings, and from my stockings into my shoes. Vhy, in my entire life, my feet have *never* touched the ground!"

Dora came up with the idea of naming my mother Goddess. My mother never forgave her.

Like almost all the Pollikoffs, Aunt Dora was brilliant. She spoke six languages, and before women had the vote she had graduated both from university and from medical school, after which she never practiced medicine a day in her life.

She married a first cousin. Most of the Pollikoffs married cousins, as they did not think anyone else was good enough for them. This particular first cousin was a rascal named Eli Pollack, who was both unfaithful and a crook.

They had a house in New York that took up an entire city block, and two children, my cousins Dale and Roy. Dale was a brilliant engineer and Roy was a brilliant doctor. Shortly after Roy was born, Eli left my aunt Dora for another woman. She never divorced him, though, because of the children. By the time I stayed with Aunt Dora, the children were in their fifties, but she told me that she and her husband, Eli, simply had a trial separation.

My mother had heard from her sister Dora all the stories about when the family had money, but she had experienced only an impecunious existence. All her sisters, my mother proclaimed, had married for love and all of them now were as poor as church mice. Thus my mother determined and announced to anyone who cared to listen that she, unlike her sisters, would marry for money. She wanted a rich old man. The richer and older the better. Preferably he would be someone in ill health whom she could help to die happy.

It was the Depression, after all. Times were tough and my mother, in growing up with the Pollikoffs, had basically grown up in a Chekhov play about exiled, charming, and useless nobility gone to ruin.

Goddess was determined to get what she wanted. And she wanted a rich old man.

She and her sisters, Ann, Emma, and Sara, and their respective husbands moved out to California. Drop-dead beautiful, my mother was the only one who was not married. In the midst of the Depression, she had a good job. Did I say good? She had a great job! Chief buyer of children's shoes at a leading department store, she made almost a hundred a week!

Goddess lived with her sister Sara and my uncle Joe and their two children, Betty-Rose and Gene. She paid them room and board, slipped her other two sisters something as well, and still had plenty left over. She had the world by the ass and at thirty years of age was regarded as the rich spinster aunt.

Someone said that she should come to the mixer at the bar of the beachfront hotel. Who knew? Maybe she would meet someone.

My father, who never drank, was drunk when he met her. She was not only the best-looking woman in the room but, he thought, one of the most beautiful women he'd ever seen.

Bald, barrel-chested, forty-four but looking fifty, with calloused hands and a thick Russian Jewish accent, he approached her.

"Can I buy you a drink?" he asked.

"No, thanks," she said and turned her back on him.

He circled around for another assault. "Sure, I buy you a drink," he said.

Well, she thought, *he is persistent.* She would soon put a stop to that.

"All right," she said. "You can buy me a drink. But just to make sure you don't think there's anything between us, which there isn't and never will be, you have to buy my friends a drink, too."

"Sure, I buy," said Papa. "Who are the friends?"

Whereupon Goddess looked him square in the eye and said, "Honey, everyone in here is my friend." She smiled and prepared to walk away, having put the foreigner in his place whereupon my father pulled out the wad. It was his life's savings, three thousand dollars in 1939, which he kept on him because he was afraid to leave it in his hotel room. To my mother it looked like pocket change. "Drinks from the house!" my father said and put a crisp hundred-dollar bill on the bar.

"What did you say your name was again, honey?" my mother asked sweetly.

"Abrash," said my dad.

"Goddess," she replied.

You bet, he must have thought.

He bought her a drink.

He brought the friends a drink. And then another, and another, and before long the whole room wanted to know who the rich Russian was who'd just bought three rounds for about 150 people.

He proposed to her that night.

"You're drunk," she told him.

"So give me the phone number and I'll call again and propose tomorrow ven I'm sober."

She gave him her number and for dinner he took her out to the Avalon Casino on Catalina Island. He showed up with a dozen long-stemmed red roses for her and a dozen for her sister Sara, who told my mother that if she were single Goddess wouldn't stand a chance.

He took her out nine times in nine days and each time proposed to her.

"I can't marry you," she said. "I don't know anything about you."

"Vat's to know?" he replied. "I'm a vorking man."

Yeah, right, she thought, *with three grand walking-around money in your pocket.* Still, he didn't seem to be a crook like the one her sister had married.

"You have relatives in Canada, friends maybe?" my father innocently asked.

"Yes," said my mother.

"So," said Papa, "I vas in business vit mine brother for many years. You ask who the brother is and you know who I am."

Well, technically it wasn't a lie. He had been in business with his brother. He had worked for him as a ranch hand. Of course by that time Uncle Hyman was a millionaire, one of the most successful cattle ranchers in western Canada. Her friends checked out Uncle Hyman. Their advice regarding my father? GRAB HIM! If he's half as rich as his brother, GRAB HIM!

But still my mother was not convinced. Then a curious thing happened that I suppose is the reason why my brother and I were born. My father enjoyed hunting, but rifles were expensive in Canada because of the tax on them. At that time, if you had been out of the country long enough you could bring up to six rifles back to Canada from the States, tax free. By chance, my father went to a sporting-goods store owned by good friends of my uncle Joe and aunt Sara, with whom my mother lived. Equally by chance, they came over for dinner. The dinner conversation went something like this:

"You'll never believe what a day we had in our store today. Christmas in the middle of summer! I'm telling you, Christmas! What kind of Christmas? This bald Russian Jewish cowboy comes in, takes a look around, and says, 'Vat's dat?' A Winchester .30-06, I say, and he says, 'I'll take it.' Doesn't ask the price, doesn't even look at it, just, 'I'll take it. Dat? I'll take it.' Six rifles! Six rifles! I'm telling you! Cash! No checks! No shmecks. I tell him the price and he doesn't even bat an eye. 'I'll take it.' Christmas!"

My mother had been silent but then cleared her throat.

"Did you happen to get his name?" she asked.

"Abrash," said the friend. "Yeah, that was it—Abrash or Abrasha. Something like that, you know it's like Abe except Russian."

My mother told the friend that this was the man who had been asking to marry her all week.

The friend looked at my mother and pronounced the sentence that closed the deal. "Goddess," she said, looking my mother square in the eye, "Goddess, Americans spend when they don't have. But Europeans? Never!"

My father told my mother that he had to go back to Canada on business, which was absolutely true. He had blown most of the three grand, was out of work, and had to find a job. He needed to know if she would marry him or not.

She said yes.

When Papa got back to Canada, he wrote and asked what kind of engagement ring she would like, white gold or yellow. My mother sent back a one-word telegram: "Platinum."

So my dad went into hock and sent her a platinum ring with a decent stone.

My mother quit her job and gave away all her possessions to her nieces.

"Your rich old-maid aunt," she told them, "is going to glory!"

My father met her at the train station and took her to the rooming house where he lived. The rooming house was the Victorian mansion of an elderly couple who had fallen on hard times. Eight bedrooms, eight baths, with stained-glass windows.

"It's not much," my father said, "but it's where I live."

My mother thought it would do just fine.

He walked her into the rooming house; a rabbi and the wedding guests were already there, waiting. My mother asked if he was out of his mind. She hadn't even had a chance to shower! She'd just gotten off the train.

"Vhat's to vait for?" my father asked innocently.

So my mother put down her suitcase, took off her hat, and got married.

It was, by all accounts a lovely wedding reception. My uncle Hyman paid for it. First rate all the way. Then all the guests, except those who lived in the rooming house, went home. My mother looked at the others and said, "Why don't they leave?"

"Vhy should they leave?" said my father. "It's a celebration."

That was strange, my mother thought.

Then my father said, "Vell, let's go up to our room."

Our room? my mother thought. *What a strange way to put it.*

They went up to my father's room and then it dawned on her.

This was my father's room! It was a rooming house! A *farkakter* rooming house!

"I never lied to you," Papa said innocently. "I said I vas a vorking man and I am. I said this is vere I live and it is. Don't tell me you married me because you thought I vas rich."

My mother later told me that she had planned to get a job the next day. She couldn't go home because she was too embarrassed. She would get a job, stay a few months, and then tell her family that her husband had died. Died and left her penniless. Then she would go back to Long Beach, a freshly minted widow, and beg for her old job back. First things first, however, and the first thing was to throw my miserable father out of the room, slam the door in his face, and lock it on him. That was her mistake.

"Vhere am I supposed to go?" my father asked, not unreasonably.

"Go to a hotel. Go to hell for all I care! You four flusher!"

"But," said my father, "I pay de rent here."

"Tough luck," said my mother.

My father might have accepted doing without a wife. But he was not about to do without a night's sleep.

"I pay de rent here!" he said and kicked the door in.

Whatever happened next, they never discussed.

They were married forty-six years when my father passed away.

A few months after my brother died, my father woke up from his afternoon nap one day. He'd had a dream and said that David had come to him and kissed him. It meant he was going to die.

"I wish to hell he'd come kiss me," my mother said.

"I'm serious," my dad said.

"So am I," said my mother.

My father died a few hours later.

Many years before, my father had bought burial plots for himself and my mom. She wanted them to be buried next to her nephew Zack. When my brother died, however, I was the one who made all the arrangements. I chose a cemetery that was closer to town and that I thought was prettier. When Papa died, I suggested to my mother that we lay him to rest next to David at the closer cemetery. My mom was not thinking very clearly. She had lost her firstborn and her husband in a span of three months so she certainly couldn't be faulted.

"Your dad wanted to be buried out here," she said, referring to the plots he'd bought. "We decided this years ago and you know your father. He'd be furious."

"Yeah," I said. "But at the time you didn't know that David would go before you guys. I just think they'd both want to be together and that way when we visit the graves we can visit both of them." It seemed like one of the weirdest conversations I'd ever had. But she wouldn't be budged.

"You know your father," she said. "He'd be furious."

So we buried my dad out in Yenemsville. It was stupid but I let it slide for more than a year. Then one day I said to my mother, "What do you say we have Dad's remains interred next to David."

"What a beautiful idea," she said. "I just wish you'd thought of it before."

"I did. You didn't want to."

"Why did you listen to me? You never listen to me! So why all of a sudden when I'm a grief-stricken widow . . ."

"You're right," I said. "I never should have listened."

A week later, I had my dad reinterred next to his firstborn son. At about that time I was working on a television project with a woman who claimed to be a psychic. I thought she was nuts, but still it was a good show. She came by my office for a production meeting.

I was rambling on about things that had to do with our show and she just kept looking at me and then looking past me, behind me. It was a little weird.

"Is everything okay?" I asked.

"I'd like to tell you something," she said. "But I'm afraid you'll think I'm crazy."

"Sharon," I said, "the truth is, I think you're nutty as a fruitcake already, so fire away."

"We're not alone," she said.

"We're not?"

"No," she said.

"We seem to be alone," I said, looking around the office.

"We're not."

"Okay," I said. "Who's here?"

"There's a man," she said. "He's dark-complected and he has a beard and black hair, almost like an Indian, and he's powerfully built and he's wearing a shroud."

No one knew—not my wife or David's wife—that I had buried my brother in a shroud. At the time, I thought it was pretty funny. I thought if he was going to be a ghost he ought to look like one, and I remembered thinking how pissed off he'd be if there was life after death, to have been buried like the ghost of Christmas Past instead of in his Armani. So I buried my dark-complected, bearded, black-haired, Indian-looking brother in a shroud.

Sharon looked past me and went on. "And he's standing next to an old man," she said and described my father. "They just want you to know how much they love you and how beautiful it is where they are and how happy they are to be together."

{ Grandma Goddess }

My mother lived six years after my father's death and in many ways I think they were the happiest six years of her life, because of her grandchildren, even with the pain of losing David.

She loved all her grandchildren, but most of all she loved Adam, my youngest son, who was a little over a year old when David and Papa died. Not old enough to be sad about anything, Adam gave joy and demanded it in return. Zaki, the eldest, was brilliant and outgoing and a born storyteller, as was Grandma Goddess. Yoni, our middle son, was a rock star, a musician and actor who was born with a spotlight on him. Adam was simply Mr. Happy. He had a truly bizarre sense of humor and everything in life seemed to amuse him.

I came home one day to find my eighty-two-year-old mother down on all fours in the family room. I thought she had fallen and was trying to get up and I had started to rush to her side when I heard Adam say, "Come on, Grandma, you can do it. Kick like a mule!" She did, and they both laughed.

Zaki came up with a story, which he and I would later write as a book called *Davin*. What follows is the chapter titled "Grandma Goddess." It's not fiction. It's my mom and the way she was with her grandchildren. Word for word.

Grandma Goddess was coming for the weekend. For Yoni and Adam and their cousin Danielle, who was staying with them for two weeks

47

that summer, that meant there would be treats from Grandma God-dess's purse. Grandma Goddess never came without treats. They were little things, little teeny tiny treasures of the kind that only grandmas notice and get for their grandchildren. There might be a toy horse for Danielle's collection, an action figure for Yoni to have adventures with, a book for Zaki, and for Adam there were always strange things because, well . . . Adam was strange.

He was four years old. Zaki was eleven. Yoni was eight and Dan-ielle, their cousin, was almost ten. One night when Adam's mother and father were putting him to bed, they gave him a big steaming cup of hot chocolate as a special treat, even though they knew he would be up before long going to the bathroom. He blew on the hot chocolate three times to cool it off and then took a big noisy slurpy sip. Then he smacked his lips and said, "Ahhhh," quite content-edly.

Then as his mother and father were kissing him good night and saying Good night, sleep tight, don't let the bedbugs bite, Adam said, "There aren't any bedbugs on Mars."

Adam's father looked at Adam's mother and Adam's mother looked at Adam's father and then they both looked at Adam.

"What do you mean?" asked Adam's father.

"About what?" said Adam innocently.

"What do you mean, there aren't any bedbugs on Mars?"

"Well," said Adam quite reasonably, "there aren't."

"But what does that have to do with you and with us saying good night to you?" asked Adam's mother.

"Well," said Adam, "that's where I live."

"Where?" said his father.

"On Mars," Adam said. And then he explained, "Every night after you kiss me good night and turn out the lights I go up to Mars."

"Uh-huh," said Adam's father. "And how do you get there?"

"In my bed," said Adam, as if his father were foolish to even ask.

"And what do you do there?" Adam's mother asked.

"I have a job," said Adam very proudly.

"Really," said his mother. "What's your job?"

"I lock up," Adam said. "I have a key and I lock up."

Adam's mother and father laughed. They told the story many times to many people and all of them laughed, too. Adam didn't care for that at all.

It seemed they were making fun of him and his job and his key. But when Grandma Goddess came for a visit shortly thereafter, she didn't laugh. Besides, she had a present.

"What is it?" Adam said.

"Open it up and you'll see," said Grandma Goddess.

Adam tore open the wrapping paper and found a little box. He opened the box and found a piece of cotton. He pulled up the piece of cotton and found a keychain. Attached to the keychain was a little tag. It was leatherette or maybe even plastic and it had white words printed on it.

"What's it say?" asked Adam excitedly.

"It says," said Grandma Goddess, putting her arm around him and sitting next to him on his bed, "'Key to Mars.'"

Adam looked at Grandma Goddess and said, "Cool."

No one could ever tell for sure how Grandma Goddess knew to bring the key. She and Adam had a secret language which only they shared. By the time Adam was five he was in love with the game of basketball and he would spend hours with Grandma Goddess watching Lakers games together with her on the phone. Before that, Grandma Goddess had not seen an entire basketball game in her life. But after Adam began to play that year, she never missed a game, and many times, past eighty years of age, she had to be restrained from going after the referee who had just called a foul on her grandson.

It was never a good idea to mess with Grandma Goddess.

Now there were two things that Zaki and Yoni and Adam and Danielle looked forward to most, every time Grandma Goddess came to visit. Pinch cookies and stories.

Pinch cookies were made of dough and had chocolate chips in them and you rolled the dough into balls and then pinched it between your fingers until it looked like a Hershey's kiss and then you baked them and they were better than anything.

Stories were what Grandma Goddess read at bedtime. Bedtime stories with Grandma Goddess could not begin until you were in jammies, in your bed with your favorite blankie, a steaming cup of hot chocolate with a marshmallow floating on top and, possibly, a pinch cookie or two.

Danielle's favorite blanket was her dribble blanket because it had things she called dribbles sewn into it that you could stick between your toes and they felt good in bed at night as you were falling asleep. It was a baby blanket but she loved it long after she had grown into a little girl. At home she tucked it under her comforter and she always brought it with her when she slept at her cousins' house.

Yoni had his blankie, which he sometimes held around his neck like a cape pretending to be a superhero. Adam had his Dallas Cowboys blanket but more important to him by far was his key to Mars, which he slept with every night.

All the children had their hot chocolate in their special mugs. Adam had his happy-as-a-clam mug. It was green and there was a smiling clam in the bottom that you could see only after you had drunk everything inside. Danielle had her pony mug. It was bright yellow and it had horses. Zaki had a big-boy mug and Yoni had his monster mug. It had a monster. There were five pinch cookies on a plate, one for each of them and one for Grandma Goddess.

"What are you gonna read, Grandma Goddess?" Adam asked impatiently.

"Hold on there, boy," Grandma Goddess said as she lowered herself into one of the tiny chairs in Adam's room. "Crime-initly."

Crime-initly was something Grandma Goddess said in the same way that other people would say Jiminy Christmas. No one ever knew what it meant.

Grandma Goddess didn't even know what it meant nor did Yoni, or Zaki, or even Adam's father, who was, after all, Grandma Goddess's son.

The closest thing they could all figure out was that "Crime-initly" was really "Crime in Italy," though why it should matter to Grandma Goddess that there was crime in Italy and why she should want to share that concern with her grandchildren was anyone's guess. To the best of anyone's knowledge, Grandma Goddess had never been to Italy and the only Italian food she liked was pizza and spaghetti. It was just something she said and it seemed to make sense.

"Crime-initly," Grandma Goddess said, "I'm an old lady, just let me sit down."

She pulled out a book that none of them had ever seen before. It looked old and worn and it was called Davin—The Secrets of the Bear.

Grandma Goddess opened the book as if she were about to read and then looked up and her voice went very soft and very low.

"I don't know," she said, "if I should read this to you or not. It could be . . . scary."

"It's not gonna be scary, Grandma Goddess," said Adam. He took another noisy sip from his hot chocolate and then looked up at her with a frightened expression in his eyes and said, "Is it?"

"I have an idea," Yoni said. "Let's turn out some lights."

And so they did. They turned out the lamp on the bookshelf and it got darker. They turned off the lamp that sat in the corner and it got darker still. Then Grandma Goddess moved in closer toward the lamp on the night table near Adam's bed. She opened the book and began to read. . . .

In the autumn of my mother's eighty-third year she died. We'd had her out to the house for a weekend that was full of activity. She had gone to an award ceremony for Zaki and then seen him off to his prom. She had seen Yoni star in a youth theater musical and had gone to one of Adam's basketball games, where she got into yet another altercation with the ref. She looked a little tired when I put her in a limo to take her home.

I called her the next morning and said I was a little worried. I was afraid we'd worn her out.

"Are you kidding?" she said. "I wouldn't have missed a second of it for the world."

She passed away about an hour later.

She was sitting on the couch, in her robe, with her feet up on the coffee table. There was a cup of tea next to her and on her lap an open photograph album of her grandchildren. Her head lay back against a pillow; her eyes were closed. She looked like a queen who had just dozed off . . . and she was smiling.

I know without any doubt that David had just kissed her.

Though not a day goes by that I do not think of my mother and smile at some sweet memory, she has not sent me any particular postcards. I have been asked why I think that is the case. The answer is so simple really. There was never a need for one. Everyone who was ever lucky enough to have been loved by my mother knew without doubt that her love would live on long after she was no longer on the planet.

{ Reb Yisrael
Ben Shmuel Dov }

When my father announced to his father that he intended to become a Zionist, to participate in the revival of Lashon Hakodesh—the holy language, Hebrew—as a spoken language rather than one reserved for communion with God, and to go rebuild the Jewish homeland with his own hands rather than wait for the Messiah, his father, Rabbi Shmuel Dov, hit him—beat him, to be exact—with his belt. Then he made my father kiss his hand so that God should grant him the strength to beat him again should the necessity arise, as it most surely would. My father took his beating, kissed his father's hand, and then said, "Fine, but I'll be the one to go to Jerusalem and make Kaddish (the mourner's prayer for the departed) over *your* father's grave." I don't know if his father hit him again. I assume he did. That came easily on that side of my family.

My father's grandfather, the Blinder Rebbe, the one over whose grave my father swore to make Kaddish, had moved to the Holy Land at an advanced age and lived another twenty or thirty years (depending on who told the story) as a famous rabbi in Jerusalem. By 1977 my father, who was by then eighty-two years old, had still not kept his promise. But, like his grandfather before him, he had gone to live out his last years and die in the Holy Land.

At the age of seventy-five he went to Israel to retire. He had made one scouting trip before that.

He had come with my mother on a nine-day package tour. Near

the end of the tour my mother began to voice her misgivings over going to live in Israel, the subject already having been broached by my father. In addition to all the other rational arguments against their moving to Israel at their age, my mother raised the point that they knew no one there and had no family of any kind. So my father set out to see if he could change that. He set out to find his family.

Although Papa had come from a traditionally large Jewish family, only one brother and sister had made it out of Russia to Canada, my uncle Hyman and my aunt Lisa, both of whom had by now long since passed away. The other brothers and sisters, as far as my father knew, were killed by either Hitler or Stalin. He did, however, have a cousin by the name of Segal. The Segal side of the family contained both Marc Chagal, who had changed his name from Segal to the more French-sounding Chagal, and Moshe Sharet, Israel's second prime minister, both of whom were more-distant cousins than the Segal whom my father had set out to find.

This particular Segal and my father were close both in age and affection. They were both Zionists who had vowed to come rebuild the Land of Israel. They last had seen each other, as near as my father could recall, in 1919 or 1920, could be 1921, definitely not later than 1922. Thus a half century had passed since either had had any news of the other. But my father was sure that Segal was in Israel.

"You're nuts," my mother said. "Plain and push it nuts, meshuge, a meshugener, a meshugener hunt [crazy dog] with nothing but meshugas. That's how nuts."

My father smiled his little smile at her. I hated that smile. It wasn't really a smirk, but you knew that's what he was thinking. He was thinking a smirk, but it came out a little smile. He would smile at me whenever he said, "You know, son, you vill find out dat life is da best teacher, vatever you need to know it vill teach. And if you don't learn it de first time, you shouldn't vorry, because if you need it, life vill teach you again." And he would smile that little smile. Anyway, that's the smile he smiled at my mother when she said he was nuts.

"First of all," she said, "you don't even know if he's alive. You haven't seen him in fifty years."

"I have a feeling," he said, like Obi Wan sensing a disturbance in the Force. "I feel he's alive and dat he's here."

"Second," said my mother, ignoring him, "you don't know if he ever made it to Israel. He could have gone to Israel. He could have gone to America, to England, Argentina, Australia, South Africa. How do you know?"

"I know," said Papa.

"How?" said my mother. "How could you know? You don't know."

"He vas very stubborn," Papa continued. "If he said he vas going to Israel, he vas going to Israel."

"You don't know," she said. And my father smiled. "You don't even know what he looks like," she said in exasperation.

"He has red hair," said my father. "His whole family has red hair."

"He's eighty years old if he's still alive," said my mother. "He doesn't have any hair!"

"You take a nap," he said. "And I'll go find my cousin."

Papa knew the following:

A. Segal was stubborn. If Segal said he was going to Israel he was going to Israel. Therefore, Segal was in Israel.

B. Segal wasn't a socialist so he wouldn't have gone to a kibbutz. He would have gone to a city. If he went to a city he would have wanted to be a pioneer. Jerusalem was already established. Tel-Aviv was rising out of the sand dunes. Ergo, Segal would have gone to Tel-Aviv.

C. Segal, outside of wanting to go to Israel, didn't like to move from place to place. Therefore, he was still in Tel-Aviv.

D. Segal had red hair.

Papa went outside and hailed a cab. He told the driver to take him to the old part of town, where the old-timers still had their shops. The cabbie took him to a part of Tel-Aviv that was one of the old neighborhoods that had not yet been gentrified. Papa paid him and walked from shop to shop. He was looking for his cousin, he explained. Came here fifty years ago, stubborn, red hair, from Poltava, you couldn't miss him. Zip in the jewelry store, nothing in the corner market or the tailor, bupkiss in the bookstore. Then someone suggested he try the barbershop.

Of course! Barbers know everything! Everything and everybody. He went to a little barbershop that had been in the same spot for fifty years. The barber was a little old man not unlike my father. He was in the middle of giving a haircut to a young customer but agreed to hear my father out. Papa launched into the description: Segal from Poltava, came in 1919, maybe 1920, could be 1921, no later than 1922, stubborn, red hair, you couldn't miss him.

"Never heard of him," said the barber.

"You're sure?" my father asked.

"Why shouldn't I be sure?" the barber answered.

My father turned around to leave.

That's when the customer spoke up. The customer was in his early forties, so my father had not directed his query to him. "Excuse me," said the customer. "You say this fellow was from Poltava?"

"That's right," said my father.

"And he had red hair?" asked the customer.

"The whole family had red hair," Papa said, beginning to think he might be onto something.

"And he would have come to Israel in the early twenties?"

"Twenty-two at the latest. Could have been twenty-one, maybe twenty, not earlier than nineteen," said Papa.

"Well," said the customer, "there's a guy in my reserve unit . . ."

"His name is Segal?" asked my father, not without some excitement.

"No," said the customer. "But he married a girl named Segal, and her grandfather came in the twenties. . . ."

"She's stubborn?"

"Like a rock," he said. "Did I say like a rock? Forget a rock," he said. "A rock is reasonable compared to this woman."

"A redhead?" my father asked.

"The whole family."

"That's him!"

By the time my mother awoke from her nap, Papa was back at the hotel, telling her to get dressed, something nice.

"Why?"

They were going out to dinner with Segal . . . and the rest of his family.

Later that night they walked into a restaurant in one of the older parts of town, and easily fifty people of four generations crowded around my father and mother. Segal had established a whole clan. Now in his early eighties and as bald as my father, Segal embraced the cousin he hadn't seen in more than half a century.

"Abrash," he said. "You haven't changed a bit!"

Five years later, my father asked me to locate his grandfather's grave.

"How would I do that?" I asked. We didn't know for sure when he'd come to Israel or when he'd died, or where he had lived, outside of the fact that he lived in Jerusalem, or *if* he even lived in Jerusalem! The whole thing could have just been a story.

"Take an afternoon," my father said. "I don't have the energy anymore."

Papa and I had traveled an odd road together. He was a violent man with a violent temper. By the time I was big enough to hit him back I was afraid I'd kill him because he was fifty-two years older than I and had already had a heart attack. That's when I left home for the kibbutz. It was, of course, mainly because of him, because of the stories I'd heard, or perhaps it was because I took some small joy in doing what he'd always wanted to do but had never done.

By now I had already served in the army, and in the reserves I had met the sons of men with whom he had fought half a century before, who were now in the same platoon with me. I was married and had a son and was working three jobs to make ends meet, and Papa wanted me to take an afternoon off to find the grave of his grandfather, over whom he'd sworn to say Kaddish as a way of getting back at the father he had defied.

I went to Jerusalem. I figured that if Papa's grandfather had come to Israel in the late 1880s, maybe 1890s, no later than the turn of the century, he would have lived either in the Old City or Mea Shearim, where the ultra-Orthodox lived, which was one of the oldest communities of the "New" City. The Jewish Quarter of the Old City had been destroyed by the Jordanians in 1948 as a way of ethnically cleansing the Jews out of that part of Jerusalem in which they had lived without a break for almost three thousand years. After the Six-Day War, in 1967, the Jewish Quarter was rebuilt, but my guess was that there would remain not so much as a shadow of remembrance of Der Blinder Rebbe in that part of town. So I went to Mea Shearim instead.

Mea Shearim, which means 'a Hundred Gates,' is a step back into medieval times. It's a European shtetl, a world of mystics and poor pious folks, of zealots and fanatics, simpletons, fools, story-tellers, and saints; a Chagal painting come to life, divided up into smaller neighborhoods, each one centering around its own sect and its own rabbi.

I stopped people in the alleyways. I'm a Jew, I said, looking for my great-grandfather's grave so my father can say Kaddish for him. Rabbi Yisrael Ben Shmuel Dov, Av Bet Din Kabalyeke, Chief Justice of the Rabbinical Court of Kabalyeke, somewhere near Poltava, Russia, at the time of the czars, Der Blinder Rebbe.

"So," said one Hassid, "you should go to the Chevre Kadisha, the burial society of the Lubavechers."

"Why?"

"Because the Lubavecher Hassidim had the strongest community back then. He could be a Belzer, but not if he's from Poltava. From Poltava? Back then? A Lubavecher."

I asked directions and he told me. I got lost and someone else told me. I got closer and another Hassid walked me up the stairs of the crumbling stone building and said, "This Jew wants to find the Lubavecher Chevre Kadisha."

Then he left me with an elderly Hassid who looked me up and down and said, "Nu?"

I told him about my great-grandfather. I told him about my father.

"Azoy," he said, which is like an Italian saying allora.

"Azoy," he said and nodded his head up and down. "So if the great-grandfather was a famous rabbi . . . he would have been buried in the Portion of the Righteous."

"Where's that?" I asked.

"On the Mount of Olives, right across from the Kotel, from the Western Wall of the Holy Temple, may it be rebuilt speedily and in our time, when the Messiah comes, Amen!"

Except he didn't say amen. He said omeyn!

Omeyn is a sound that has flesh on its bones. It smells of schmaltz, of herring, of old men in synagogues, swaying in their prayers, punctuating them with a sound that is to Hassidim what "Hallelujah" is to Pentecostals.

"Omeyn!" he said, and took down a very dusty leather-bound book that was, he said, over a hundred years old. It smelled the smell of old bindings and glue and paper ready to return to dust, and dust itself.

"So," he said, and began running his finger down the columns written in tiny handwriting with swirls and the flourishes of another age.

I lit a cigarette. Such things were not considered rude in those days.

"Make a glass tea," he said as his finger slid down one column and then started a new journey up the next.

"That's okay," I said. "I'm not thirsty."

"For me," he said, without looking up.

"Oh."

"Yeah, oh," he said.

I took the electric teakettle, the *kum kum,* filled it with water from an ancient squeaky tap, and plugged it in. There was a cupboard and bound files and pencils, carbon paper, fiche, and Vysotsky Tea. I took down a glass with a delicate little metal holder, feminine almost in its design. I snuffed out the cigarette, put in the tea bag, and then took another glass down for myself. The old Hassid, without even looking up, said, "Oh, so now, all of a sudden, he's thirsty."

"May I?" I asked.

"Bevakasha, bevakasha," he said. "Help yourself. What kind of person begrudges a man a glass tea?"

He licked his index finger and turned the page.

The teakettle whistled and I poured boiling water into the glasses.

"A bissel lemon," he said. "They're on the sink. You want?"

"No, thanks," I said. I cut off a slice of lemon for him.

"Two teaspoons sugar," he said. I put in the two teaspoons and stirred the tea.

"I told you tea, not coffee!" he said. "Take the tea bag out." I took the tea bag out.

"On the sink," he said.

I put the tea bag on a saucer next to another tea bag on the sink.

He blew. He sipped. He smacked his lips. He said ahhhhh, licked his index finger, and turned another dusty page.

I lit up another cigarette.

Two hours later he said, ah hah!

"What ah hah?"

"What ah hah? This ah hah! Reb Yisrael Ben Shmuel Dov, Chief Justice of the Rabbinical Court of Kabalyeke, may his memory be a blessing."

"You found it?"

"No, *you* found it! Of course I found it!"

He motioned me over to look. "*Geb ah kuk*," he said.

I looked where he pointed and saw my great-grandfather's name, a Hebrew date, and a series of numbers neatly written in beside the name, indicating the row and plot number.

"You've got a car?" he asked.

"No."

"Money for a taxi?"

"Where are we going?" I asked as he took me by the arm and headed for the door, bundling the old leather-bound book up and tucking it under his arm and grabbing his hat.

Outside and down below the street that existed in another time, we walked up one alleyway, cut across another, through a vacant lot where a rooster strutted and forlocked children ran and shouted at each other in Yiddish, and finally out to a larger street, one that lived in the twentieth century, unlike the ones from the Chagal painting that we had just left behind. We hailed a taxi.

"Har Ha Zeitim," he said to the driver. "To the Mount of Olives."

This was long before the intifadah, and a Jew in East Jerusalem had nothing to fear. Later, this same trip would get you killed.

"Now the question," he said, was " . . . is there anything left of the grave?"

He explained that in 1948, after the fall of the Old City, the Jordanians not only expelled all the Jews and destroyed the Jewish Quarter, they also put a road through the holiest Jewish cemetery on earth, the one on the Mount of Olives. They used the grave markers for paving stones. There was a good chance, he said, instead of your great-grandfather's grave, we'll find the Jordanian road.

We got up to the Mount of Olives just before sunset. The Portion of the Righteous was located down from the Intercontinental Hotel. We passed a camel tied up next to a photographer. The camel was there for the tourists. You paid the photographer a few pounds and he put a *kaffiyeh*, or Arab headdress, on you and sat you on the camel for the *Lawrence of Arabia* shot. The Intercontinental catered to mainly Christian tour groups and the camel and the headdress were a great hit for many years.

A series of stone steps led to a low stone wall that encircled the main part of the cemetery. All the original gravestones had been torn up or broken. New ones had been set up in their places here and there.

These were new graves of newly dead and new gravestones of the long since dead.

In the Portion of the Righteous, however, very few stones were intact. These were the graves of people who had died so long ago that all who mourned them were dead and buried themselves.

The old Hassid was looking for a name on a stone, any name, any stone, so that he could get his bearings. Then he found one: Katzin. He opened up the dusty leather-bound book and pulled out a plot map, located the name on the plot map, looked around the graveyard, and made his mental calculations.

"Katzin," he said. "Here is Katzin in the book. And here is Katzin's stone," he said, pointing to the gravestone he had found. "Your great-grandfather is three rows up and six stones to the left."

I looked up. The third row up from ours was the last row before the Jordanian road. I leaped up over Katzin's gravestone to the third row and counted six across to the left. There it was, the foundation of the grave of my great-grandfather, Rabbi Yisrael Ben Shmuel Dov.

A month later I stood with my father in front of the newly erected stone we had put up and together with him prayed the mourner's prayer over the dead. I had seen my father cry only once before in his life, which was when he got the news that his brother Hyman had died.

He wept and I put my arm around him. My father cried, but not for my great-grandfather, whom he did not know, whom he had never met. He cried for all that had come between his father and him. He cried for hating him; he cried for loving him. He cried for not loving him enough. He cried for his father's love and all the years he'd spent without it. That's what we buried that day, his bitterness, and right alongside it, mine.

"Oh, Grant Peace," the words of the Kaddish say. "He will grant peace upon us and all of Israel, and let us say, Amen."

Finding my great-grandfather's grave was, I believe, a postcard. One that healed my father . . . and me.

{ ZAKI }

Zaki Gordon was blessed with almost everything—talent, wit, beauty, a fair and sunny disposition, wisdom far beyond his years, an enormous capacity to love and accept love, an ability to enjoy all that life had to offer, and the gifts that enabled him to offer something back to life. He was blessed with everything . . . except the gift of years. He walked this earth for twenty-two glorious summers and left a legacy that increases in size and strength with each passing year.

When he was born he was called an old soul, and I believe that to be true. I have come to believe that he simply didn't have much left to do on this earth and so his stay was all too brief.

He had to fight to be born at all and he made it clear that he was not even a little bit happy about that. His mother was in labor for twenty hours in Hadera's Assaf Harofeh Hospital in Israel. The umbilical cord was wrapped twice around his neck and it took forceps and suction to bring him out. His head looked like a squashed potato, one that had been stepped on and perhaps stepped on again.

When the nurse brought him out into the waiting room, however, his eyes were completely focused and his vision stereoscopic. He looked each one of us square in the eyes and then moved on to the next one down the line and stared him down as well with a look that was absolute cold fury at what he had just gone through.

The nurse, who was Moroccan, was so unnerved by Zaki's look that she spit three times and made the sign against the evil eye. She had been a nurse for twenty years, she said, and had never seen a look like that before. Zaki was born, and he was pissed. Perhaps, recognizing that he had been born into a Jewish family in Israel, he realized that he was only a week away from being circumcised as well.

Papa was going to be his godfather as well as his grandfather. He would be the one not only chosen to spoil him but the one who would be responsible for his spiritual life, indeed his spirit itself. We lived in Israel until Zaki was four and then moved back to the United States.

When Zaki was six years of age I went to Israel to work on a film I was writing. I called home from Tel-Aviv, in those days a very expensive long-distance call. When Zaki got on the phone with me he was very excited. "Abba," he said (Abba means Daddy in Hebrew), "I made up a movie!"

"That's wonderful," I told him. "I can't wait to hear it when I get home."

"But I've got to tell you now," he said, in his very serious six-year-old's voice. He was not disappointed, not sulking, neither petulant nor pouting, simply serious, man-to-man sort of serious.

I told him, with equal seriousness, that he really didn't have to tell me now and that it could wait until I got home, this being a very expensive long-distance call. I knew, moreover, that Zaki did not know any short stories. His were long and involved and had characters with accents and sound effects, scene settings and at times theme songs, if not full-blown musical scores.

But Zaki insisted that he had to tell me now.

One of the ways in which Zaki was remarkable was that, almost from birth, when he saw the logic of something you'd explained, he would comply with whatever parental dictum you had just laid down. He even acquiesced to the last-resort explanation: that, being the parent, this was my best judgment and, being the child, he would just have to trust that judgment until he was old enough to make those judgments for himself, which in no case could be before he turned eighteen and was financially independent, whichever came later. If he didn't agree or thought he was being treated unfairly, he would note it for the record and explain the logic of his position and give you a look that said clearly he would, out of love, indulge, but not forget, your wrongheadedness.

On this occasion I had not yet resorted to the "because I'm your father routine" and so Zaki pressed on with his logic. "I can't wait until you get home to tell the story," he said. "If I could I would, but I can't, so I've got to tell you now."

"All right," I said. "If you can tell me why you can't wait until I get home and it makes sense, then you can tell me now. But if not, you've got to wait till I get home. Okay?"

"I think that's fair," he said, reasonably.

"Well, I'm glad," I said. "So . . . why can't you wait to tell me the story until I get home?"

Without pausing for an instant he replied, "I can't wait because I don't know how to write yet and by the time you get home I might forget it, so I have to tell you now."

"Realizing that there was no way to fault that line of thinking, I said, "I guess you do."

For roughly the next forty-five minutes, Zaki told me the most beautiful children's story I had ever heard, complete with accents, sound effects, scene settings, and what he admitted was a borrowed theme song.

When I got back to Los Angeles I told my agent, Jerry Zeitman, to set up a meeting with Amblin, Steven Spielberg's company.

I pitched Zaki's story, which was called *Davin,* to Spielberg's development person. She liked it a lot. That evening I came home with no small amount of excitement. My six-year-old was on the verge of a deal with Steven Spielberg.

"Did they like it?" he asked as I walked in the door.

"They loved it," I said. "Steven Spielberg's company wants to make your movie!"

"They do?"

"They do," I said.

"And did they like the part about Princess Helen?" he asked.

"Absolutely."

"And the Bugle Boy and El Lobo, the greatest swordsman in Spain?"

"They ate it up."

"Cool," he said.

"Now," I said, "let me tell you their notes."

"Notes?" Zaki asked. It was a term with which he was not unfamiliar.

"Their changes," I said, cutting to the chase.

"What do you mean, changes?" he asked.

"There are things they want to change," I said.

He looked at me very evenly and spoke to me as if I were a child, and a slow-witted one at that.

"But if they change it," he said, "then it won't be my story anymore."

"Sure it will," I said. "It will be your story with their changes."

He just looked at me.

"It'll still be your story," I said lamely.

"No," said the six-year-old author, speaking what we both knew was the absolute truth. "It won't."

Now I thought it was my turn to speak the absolute truth.

"Sweet boy," I said, "the truth is, if we make the changes, they'll pay me a lot of money and I'll write the screenplay and they might make the movie. If we don't make the changes, they won't pay me any money and I won't write the screenplay and they won't make the movie."

"If they change it," he said, "it's not my story."

Okay, if he was going to simply restate his position, I'd do the same.

"We make the changes, they pay the money, I write the screenplay, they might make the movie," I said, looking into his very old-soul beautiful eyes. "On the other hand, no changes, no money, no screenplay, no movie. You're way too young to have to learn that, but that is, unfortunately, the truth."

"I see," he said, and I could see that he did. He was quiet. Then he looked up at me and said again, "I see." Then he said, "What would you recommend that we do?"

"The truth?" I asked.

He nodded his head, bracing himself for the truth I was about to speak.

"I'd make the changes," I said, never looking away from his eyes.

He was quiet again and then said, "All right . . . fine." Then he looked directly into my eyes and said, "You do that on one of *your* projects, not mine."

I picked up the phone, called my agent, and said, "Tell Amblin we don't have a deal. We're pulling the project."

"Why?" asked my agent.

"My partner won't agree to the changes."

After I hung up I told Zaki that when he was older, the two of us would write the story as a book, and we wouldn't make any changes.

And that's what we did. When he was in his sophomore year in college we wrote *Davin* together. I would write a draft and send it to him and he would rewrite me and then send the draft back to me and I would rewrite him, until neither of us could tell anymore who had written what. Delacorte Press published it in hardcover. Zaki was a published author in hardcover at nineteen years of age.

Some years before that, however, when Zaki was sixteen, he overheard me telling someone about how he had not agreed to make the changes Amblin requested and thus we had passed on the deal with Steven Spielberg. Later that evening he pulled me aside.

"Let me ask you something," he said.

"Shoot," I answered.

"Was that a true story?" he asked.

"Was what a true story?" I replied.

"The thing about Spielberg. About how we had a deal with Amblin on *Davin.*"

"True story," I said.

"Not embellished?"

"Not even a little bit."

"We had a deal with Steven Spielberg . . ." he said.

"Yep."

"AND YOU BLEW IT BECAUSE OF A SIX-YEAR-OLD!" he exploded. "ARE YOU OUT OF YOUR MIND?"

Zaki did his first two years of university at Columbia. Not exactly a slouch school. Sometime in his second semester there, when freshmen were flunking out in droves he asked, "When does it get hard?"

For Zaki it never did.

It was effortless for him and that fact embarrassed him. I asked him about his grades at Columbia and he said, "Well, grades, you know, what can I tell ya?"

"You can tell me," I said, "what your grades are." I was paying for his education at that Ivy League school and felt I had a right to know.

Zaki looked at me philosophically and then smiled.

"I never really look at grades as an indication of how well I'm doing," he said, with a kind of lazy grace of which one is either capable at birth or not. Incapable of such elegance, I pressed on.

"You don't look at grades as an indication of how well you're doing?"

"No," he said, smiling softly and shaking his head.

"What do you think your grades are an indication of?" I asked.

"I generally think of them as a kind of test of whether or not the professor can spot talent, intelligence, wit, that sort of thing. Sometimes, I must admit, they disappoint me."

He never did tell me what his grades were. The university, in its wisdom, sent report cards to him without copying either of his parents.

Well, I thought, *they're still sending me bills for his tuition so he couldn't have flunked out.*

After completing his first two years at Columbia, Zaki transferred into NYU's Tisch School of the Arts as a film major. That particular film school is rightly regarded as the most difficult one in the country into which to gain entry. His grades had to be fairly decent, I reasoned.

I tried once again, in vain, to get some inkling of Zaki's scholastic standing once he was enrolled in NYU. I fared no better than I had when he was at Columbia.

Finally, his mother and I received confirmation that he was going to graduate, and both of us heaved a big sigh of relief.

It was only at his graduation exercise, when I read the program, that I learned what his scholastic achievement had been. He was graduated from NYU summa cum laude, the highest academic honor the university could bestow.

Zaki slept through the ceremony. It bored him.

Somewhere in Zaki's sophomore year the university decided it was going to cut back on its affirmative-action program. The students protested the administration's decision and the protest found its ultimate expression in the decision of several students to stage a hunger strike.

There was to be a student rally in the auditorium to encourage the hunger-striking students in their protest.

Zaki wanted to go to the rally in solidarity with several of his friends who were among the hunger strikers. Included among them was Zaki's roommate, an African American student whose nickname was Twig. About six foot six, Twig was on the basketball team. Zaki was barely five foot seven. He was not on the basketball team. They were best friends. Mutt and Jeff.

Twig had promised to save Zaki a seat in the front row since Zaki had a test to take and would be coming late. Zaki finished his test and rushed off for the rally. It was past one o'clock in the afternoon and Zaki had not had any breakfast that day and was starving.

He reasoned, quite rightly, that they wouldn't be serving anything to eat at a hunger strike, so he thought the only thing to do was to pick up a bite on the way to the rally. He bought a falafel from a street vendor and then became engrossed in a conversation with a fellow student on the way to the auditorium. Being thus engaged in conversation, he forgot to eat the falafel he was holding, and realized he was still holding it only as he took his seat in the first row of the auditorium. The smell of fried chickpeas, hummus, and tahini wafted up to the hunger strikers onstage.

Of course, Zaki was embarrassed.

The only thing to do, he reasoned, was to finish the falafel, which by now was clearly distracting the famished protestors, as quickly as he could. He began gobbling up the dripping Middle Eastern delicacy.

Tahini dripped onto his forearm.

He licked it off.

The hunger strikers drooled, salivated, swooned.

Zaki ate faster, making what he described as Cookie Monster sounds as he devoured the falafel.

Some of the hunger strikers onstage began to turn ugly.

Twig turned to his much shorter friend and said, "Yo, you better get outta here with that falafel drippin' down your arm like that, man."

Zaki decided that Twig had a point. He got up, to a growing chorus of hisses and boos, just as the speaker onstage was exhorting his comrades to take no more from "the man," rather to take to the streets in protest.

By now Zaki had reached the back of the auditorium.

He flung open the doors just as the crowd surged behind him.

He finished the last bite of falafel but there was still tahini dripping down his forearm. So he raised his fist, clenched around the falafel wrapper, in order to get a better shot at the dripping tahini.

That's when the photographer snapped the picture, which graced the front page of a newspaper the next day. There was Zaki, looking defiantly heroic, clenched fist raised in the air, being followed by the minions he was now leading out into the streets.

The caption read, "Hunger Strikers storm out in protest called by Student Activist Leader."

Zaki was the only person in the world who could bring a falafel to a hunger strike and still walk away with the best press.

{ HANUKAH }

Zaki died in a car accident at the age of twenty-two, six months after he graduated.

It is difficult for me to this day to talk or write about the accident in anything but the most cursory manner. Yet, certain things need to be said so that you can understand the postcard that I later received.

Zaki had decided to stay on living in New York after graduation. Had he come back to L.A. I could certainly have helped him get started as a writer / director in the studio part of the motion-picture industry, which is of course a large part of the reason that he stayed in New York. He didn't want my help. The truth is, he was so wonderfully talented and disciplined and charismatic that he did not need help, neither from me nor anyone else. Another part of the reason he stayed in New York was that he didn't want to be in the studio end of the business. He had seen me labor and compromise in those fields all his life and he was determined to tell his stories without the studio note system, which he knew I regarded as akin to anal rape. He was going to be a New York indie writer / director; a truly independent filmmaker.

He also simply loved New York. He loved the rain on the streets and the reflections of lights and canyons of buildings and smells and languages and sounds and energy and the way the city wouldn't let you off the hook, accosted you, demanded your attention; loved the museums and clubs and bodegas and the Met and the trains and taxis and Christmas and FAO Schwartz and the Plaza and the Blue Note and the Village and the Bowery and Tribeca and the delis and Chinatown, the goombas, the salsa, the rhythm, the beat, the clickety-clack, the winos and the cops and the bums and the stories and the music and the sway of hips and lovers in the shadows and glimpses of dramas in doorways, loved being young and in and out of love in New York.

Just after Thanksgiving and before Hanukah and Christmas, in what would be the last few weeks of his life, Zaki and I were working together in New York. Together but separately. I was in preproduction on *The Hurricane* and Zaki was working as a production assistant on an HBO movie, *Studio 54,* I think. We were both putting in long hours and neither of us got off much before midnight. There was a steak house midway between where his picture was shooting and mine was prepping. We would meet there every night at twelve thirty or one and, over steaks and a bottle of cabernet, bitch about the jerks we were working with. And I remember so vividly thinking, *This is absolutely as good as it gets.* My son and me, both working at our craft, which the two of us shared, the only two in our family who spoke that secret language and walked those secret trails and knew each other's lives, father and son, former writing partners and dearest friends. I tried to memorize the way he looked, his stories, his laughter, his youth, as if knowing that these sweet moments were in limited supply.

The movie gods smiled on both of us. Both productions were breaking for the holidays. Both of us would be able to be in California for Hanukah with Zaki's brothers, one home from college and the other still in high school. We would be together, all of us, but I remember thinking, *Let me just savor this between the two of us now, seeing him now as a young man, no longer a schoolboy, having a beer with his old man; let me just savor it, snap a photograph of the heart, tuck it away like a secret treasure, wrapped in tissue all nice and safe, to be pulled out as a keepsake someday, perhaps when he shares a steak or a beer with his own son.*

I came back to L.A. a few days before Zaki got there. Zaki's middle brother, Yoni, would arrive even later because of finals, but we would all be together for Hanukah; Zaki and his brothers, Yoni and Adam; their cousin Greg, who was a paramedic; Greg's sister Debi, who had been the boys' babysitter when they were younger and was more like a big sister than a cousin, and her husband, James; her mother, Jo-Ann; my cousins Betty and Herman, who were more like a big brother and sister; my brother's first wife, Toni, and her husband, Ed; and my nephew Brian, David's son Brian, the most conceited retarded kid you ever met in your life. Though severely mentally disabled, Brian had my brother's arrogance and capacity for fun. He thought, and thinks to this day, that he is the coolest guy around; the handsomest, funniest, most popular and most loved, and of course he's right. Whenever he comes into a room he immediately names not only all those there but those long departed as well. So, after greeting all of us and calling me Uncle Dam and saying, "Kiss!" and getting his hugs and kisses from one and all, he would call out for Grandma Goddess and Papa, both of whom had been dead for many years, but not to Brian. They were always part of the party, even though Brian was never completely sure what party it was. Thus, to cover all his bases, he greeted one and all alike with "Merry Christmas, hap' Hanukah, hap' birthday!" In this way, Brian never slights anyone of any religion, and he does not discriminate between the living and the departed. Thus it was that Brian exclaimed, "Zaki, kiss! Adam, Grandma Goddess, Papa, hap birthday, Merry Christmas, hap' Hanukah!"

My Sweetheart was there beside me, the two of us cooking the holiday meal, when we got word that Yoni's plane was delayed. He would not get in until around midnight, so we would have to go ahead without him. Zaki had just gotten in and was exhausted. There seemed to be very little left of him and he seemed so slight. My kibbutz father, who had been like the boys' grandfather after

Papa died, had said the same thing the last time he'd seen him and was clearly worried.

(Having been an "outside child" at the kibbutz when I was sixteen, I was given a kibbutz family. They became as important in my life as my biological family.)

"There's nothing left of him," he would say.

"He's a kid," I said. "He's skinny and he's putting in long hours."

But Chanan, my kibbutz father, was worried. "It's like a light getting dimmer," he said. I tended to dismiss such things from Chanan. He had a gloomy outlook on life, having lived a tragic one. He had lost his whole family in the Holocaust. His only son had been killed at sixteen, when the pickup in which he was riding flipped over on the way to a basketball game in which he was to have played. So I dismissed what Chanan had said. How could Zaki's light be getting dimmer? No one's future was as bright as his. But now, on this night of Hanukah, the Festival of Lights, I was worried as well. Zaki seemed to have diminished in only the last few days since I'd seen him in New York. I asked him if he was feeling okay.

"Just tired," he said, and then he asked what we had to drink.

"We've got beer," I said, "wine, soft drinks."

"Have anything from Kentucky or Tennessee?" he asked impishly, having evidently grown fond of Jack Daniels and the like.

"Beer and wine," I said.

"I could do wine," he said, as his cousin Debi came up and slipped her arm around him and gave him a kiss and said she liked his hair; the last time she'd seen him it was a buzz. Then she said, "Zaki, you smell like Uncle Abe."

Uncle Abe was my father, Abrash, Papa.

"I'm sorry," Zaki joked. "I'll take a shower."

But Debi was not in a joking mood. She was insistent and she said, "No really, you smell just like Uncle Abe."

I leaned in and took a whiff of my son. He didn't smell any different to me and I was not indifferent on the subject. When Zaki was little he suffered from truly terrible, at times life-threatening, asthma. More than once he had been in intensive care in hospitals in Israel and California. More than once I had prayed for my son's life to be spared, offered bargains to God, offered to trade my own life for Zaki's, offered praises and promises of anything God had in mind to waylay the Angel of Death and keep him from our door, keep him from my firstborn child, my Boy, my son. I had become aware of a sickly sweet odor that emanated from Zaki's scalp just before the onset of an asthma attack. I told his doctor this and it in fact never failed. From then on, the minute I smelled that smell on his hair, we started his medication as a prophylactic. Thus, when Debi said that he smelled like my deceased father, I immediately took a whiff. *Maybe his asthma is about to come back,* I thought, as if only asthma could do him harm. But the sickly sweet smell wasn't there.

"I don't smell anything," I said.

"Well, I do!" Debi said defiantly. "I don't know how you can say you don't smell anything. He smells just like Uncle Abe!"

Debi seemed to be getting genuinely angry about the whole thing. I tried logic. "Debi," I said, "that's silly. I don't even remember what my father smelled like."

"Well, I do!" she said, eyes flashing now in defense of the memory of my father's particular smell. "And he," she said, pointing at Zaki, "smells just like him."

"Hey, you know what?" Zaki said. "I think I'm just gonna curl up and go to sleep."

So saying, Zaki curled up on the step that led from the family room up to the door that gave out onto the backyard.

"You want to go lie down?" I asked.

But he was already curled up on the step, already half asleep. He looked like a little kitten curled up like that. Later, about the time we were giving out presents, he got his second wind. I watched him regaling his cousins with stories as my Sweetheart and cousin Betty and my brother's first wife, Toni, and I did the dishes in the kitchen. I snapped photographs of the heart.

That night, as everyone was getting ready to leave, Zaki asked, "Do you want us to stay?" I thought how sweet it was. Since I had divorced it was always a treat to have the boys under my roof, staying in the new home I had made for myself, and I wanted them to feel that this was their own as well. But the home where their mother lived was the home they'd grown up in, the one with their stuff and their memories, and moreover their brother Yoni would be coming in from the airport and would go straight over to their mother's since she had picked him up.

"No," I said. "You guys go hang with your brother and I'll see you some time tomorrow." I hugged his younger brother first. Adam is the jock of the family and even at that age his body felt solid and fit.

"I love you," I said and hugged him to me again.

"Love you, too," he said.

Then I hugged Zaki to me. It felt like there was nothing left of him. "You sure you're okay?" I asked.

"I'm just really tired," he said.

I smelled his hair. It didn't smell like asthma.

"I love you, kiddo," I said.

"I love you, too," he said.

"Drive safe," I said, and then I tossed him the keys to my SUV. It was just beginning to softly rain. Just a mist.

{ SHABBES HANUKAH }

The accident occurred the next day. Saturday. Shabbat, Shabbes, the Sabbath.

Zaki and his brothers, Yoni and Adam, were on their way from their mother's house to the mall to buy her a present for Hanukah. There was a light rain, just enough to loosen the oil on the highway and make it its most dangerous. The on-ramp, which now bears a warning and reduced-speed sign, is a particularly treacherous one; a sharp turn that twists ninety degrees and merges immediately into traffic. It is the kind of on-ramp that inspires mothers to tell their children to be quiet until a safe merge onto the freeway has been accomplished. The boys were having a fine time. They were joking. They were laughing.

There has not been a day, not an hour, since then that I have not hated myself for not having thrown my son the keys to a Volvo; one with new tires and side airbags, instead of the keys to the SUV, with the drive that was far too skittish and uneven and the tires too old, and Zaki, a New Yorker, unused to driving anymore. But regret and a few bucks will buy you a latte. Somewhere in that ninety-degree turn in the light-falling rain, the car lost traction and began to swerve, and at some point Zaki braked and at some point the car, veering out of control, collided with a fuel truck. The fuel tanker jackknifed and tipped over. The pavement ripped a hole in its side. The sparks ignited the fuel. Yoni and a passerby pulled Adam out of the SUV.

They could not get to Zaki before the flames engulfed the entire freeway, keeping any saving hands away from Zaki, who was either killed on impact or knocked unconscious. I don't know which to this day. I know only that the flames consumed everything, everything, everything. The freeway was shut down for days. An entire section had to be resurfaced as the intensity of the heat of the fire had quite simply melted the asphalt.

Yoni didn't have a scratch.

Adam didn't have a scratch.

The driver of the fuel truck didn't have a scratch.

The accident, evidently, had had nothing to do with anyone . . . but Zaki.

I do not believe that what I am about to say are the words of a bereaved father looking for comfort. As far as I'm concerned, I deserve no comfort. Nor do I seek any. But I do believe completely that there is this to be said:

If God intended to pull the soul out of a healthy young man of twenty-two years of age, and do it in such a way that that young soul, so full of life, could not try, as it probably would have, to return to the spacesuit, so to speak, God could have done no better than consume the spacesuit utterly and completely so that the young soul could not return, no matter how much it might mistakenly long to do so.

That was one. (Confession to make, I am writing this chapter with Jack Daniels as my companion.) Two: For Zaki's brothers, Yoni and Adam, there was no comfort. This was as awful a thing as any human being should ever have to go through. I cannot even write the words of what they must have had to endure in those first moments after the crash and the conflagration that followed. That is why I so give thanks to a merciful God for what happened next. The first paramedic on the scene was their cousin Greg . . . their cousin Greg, who had been with them both and their brother Zaki less than a dozen hours before, lighting the Hanukah lights. Their cousin Greg was there first and within moments, to protect them and shield them and comfort them and turn them away from the terrible sight that assailed them, to hold them and hug them and love them as an older and stronger brother and grieve with them and succor them and console them as much as any on this earth could grant them comfort.

We wept, how we wept, and told Zaki stories, his brothers, his mother, his friends, relations, and I, and somehow we laughed and smiled at the memories of the light in which we all had been bathed for twenty-two glorious summers and one autumn.

We buried him with white roses and his brother Yoni's songs, and his brother Adam's stories and his mother's and grandmother's and mine, rejoicing, truly rejoicing, and giving thanks for the hours of his life among us. And when the mourners left, in the days that followed, and when Yoni went back to school, Adam and I were left, as his mother was left, alone with our demons in California. Adam, enduring the slow torture of joint custody, spent Mondays and Wednesdays with his mother and Tuesdays and Thursdays and alternate weekends with me. God help him.

It was on the Tuesday after we buried my firstborn son that I saw the rabbit.

I work at home.

I have an office in my home with a sliding glass door that leads out into the backyard. There is a small patch of flagstone and then a small patch of grass, then a wooden deck and a hot tub (this is after all California). Then a beautiful shipwrecked tree leaning over, propped up in a steel brace and covered in morning glories, and beyond that a playhouse that served as a fort for my boys and then as a place for my youngest to practice his drums, and a pool and a fence that separates our yard from the local community park.

And so on that Tuesday after we consigned a box with Zaki's spacesuit to its real estate, on that Tuesday in my office, in my home, staring out the sliding glass door into the yard, I saw the rabbit.

It was not a white rabbit, not an Alice in Wonderland rabbit, but a jackrabbit, a skinny, gray, mousy-colored, run-of-the-mill jack-rabbit. This is important because all my life when my father, Papa, Abrash, Uncle Abe, was alive, whenever he, my father, Papa, Abrash, Uncle Abe, wanted to describe the most frightened creature imag-inable in creation, the coward, in fact of all cowards, he would say (and I can hear his Russian Jewish accent as I write this), "Vhy he vas scared as a jeckrabbit." A jeckrabbit was the same thing as a jackrab-bit. So now imagine my surprise, no, my amazement, when, looking out my office window (or sliding glass door to be exact) into the backyard, I saw, sitting perfectly still, not three feet away, staring straight up into my eyes, nothing less than . . . a jackrabbit. Now it must be said that I have had no small amount of experience with jackrabbits. I live in a place called the Conejo Valley.

Conejo is Spanish for "rabbit." The Conejo Valley isn't called the Conejo Valley because we don't have jackrabbits. We, Dear Reader, are afloat in jackrabbits. Jackrabbits indeed regard our gardens as something akin to the salad buffet at Sizzler.

Trust me, I know from jackrabbits. I have chased them, shouted at them, even, I must admit, fired BB guns at them in an attempt to protect what I laughingly call my garden. And at each of these junc-tures, the jackrabbits ran, and I stayed. That, after all, as my father knew only too well, is the nature of jackrabbits.

"Scared as a jeckrabbit," Papa would always say, "scared as a jeckrabbit." Thus, I knew, looking out the sliding glass door at the jackrabbit who stared so calmly back at me, that jackrabbits were, by nature, scared.

Except this jackrabbit wasn't.

He looked at me like he was the Dalai Lama.

Placid.

Calm.

Tranquil.

Enlightened.

At peace.

I opened the sliding glass door.

"Yo, Rabbit," I said. "Who are you?"

Now, I'm not stupid. I didn't expect the rabbit to answer me. But I did expect the rabbit to run. To run, in fact, like a jackrabbit.

The rabbit sat there and gave me his Dalai Lama look. Not scared, not mocking me, just there and peaceful, as if waiting for me to become less hysterical than I evidently was.

"You want some food?" I asked the rabbit and raced maniacally to the kitchen. I found some carrots in the fridge, brought out a bunch, and set them before the rabbit.

The rabbit just looked.

It didn't eat and it didn't run.

It just looked.

"There you go, Bugs," I said, trying to be cute. "Carrots. Go ahead. Jump in. *Es a bissell.*" I said, thinking perhaps the rabbit spoke a mixture of English and Yiddish.

"*Yalah, tochal mashehu!*" I said in a mixture of Arabic and Hebrew.

"*Mangia!*" I said, putting my fingers to my mouth in the universal gesture meaning "eat something."

The rabbit just sat there.

"Whatsa matter?" I asked. "Carrots too big?" I said in baby talk.

I broke the carrots in half, in quarters, in thirds, and set them before the rabbit, like a supplicant in prayer.

The rabbit didn't even touch them. Didn't sniff even.

"What's up?" I asked.

Obviously the rabbit didn't answer. It just sat there.

So I just sat there.

The rabbit looked at me.

I looked at the rabbit.

Then I went back inside the house.

The rabbit stayed there.

Then Adam came home.

The rabbit stayed there.

I said, "Adam, check out this crazy-assed rabbit!"

He did.

The rabbit just stayed there.

Then I asked Adam if he wanted to throw the football around. More to please me than for any other reason, I believe, he said yes.

So we went outside with the football to throw it around. The rabbit went with us.

We walked out the back gate into the park in order to have room to throw the football around.

The rabbit went with us.

We threw the football back and forth.

We ran.

We jumped.

We shouted.

And still the rabbit stayed with us, or more correctly stayed right next to Adam, and when we came back into our yard the jackrabbit came with us. And when we walked back up to the house, the rabbit walked with us. And after we went into the house and Adam went to his bedroom, I walked outside and the rabbit was still there.

"Rabbit," I asked, "did Zaki or Papa send you here?"

The rabbit twitched its nose.

I'm not claiming that it spoke to me. I'm not a fool, after all. I'm only saying this jackrabbit, this scared-as-a-jackrabbit jackrabbit, just stayed there and twitched its nose.

"Whoever sent you," I said, "please tell them thank you, and that I got the message. Zaki's okay I think, right?"

The jackrabbit twitched its nose. I felt the kind of relief only a parent knows when he knows his child has arrived safely home.

"Thanks," I said. "You can go now."

The jackrabbit left and I never saw it again. Ever.

A year later, as was the custom, we had the unveiling for Zaki's gravestone. It was only then, when I looked at Papa's gravestone, that I understood.

What did you understand, you might ask?

Well, since you asked I'll tell you. Papa's gravestone carried his date of birth as 1898.

Now, that was a lie.

Papa, my father, Abrash, Uncle Abe, was not born in 1898.

Papa, my father, was born in 1895.

He knew it. My mother knew it and I knew it. And we all knew he knew we knew it.

The DMV, on the other hand, did not know it, so Papa put his birthdate as 1898 instead of 1895.

"When it comes time," he said to me near the end of his life, "you put down de birthdate, you put it down like I'm telling you, 1898."

"But, Pop," I said, "you were born in 1895. I mean who are you trying to impress, you know? I mean, like you want people to believe you're eighty-eight instead of ninety-one?"

My father was furious. "Vat's dat?" he shouted. "De pup is telling the dog vat's vat?"

"The pup's not tellin' the dog anything," I said. "I'm just saying . . ."

"And I'm telling you," my father thundered. "You put it down de vay I say! You hear? You put it down 1898! Dat's de vay it's got to be! You hear me? Dat's de vay it's got to be!"

"Okay," I said. "Okay. That's the way it's got to be, then that's the way it's got to be. Done. I'm cool."

So when Papa died I had put on his stone 1898 instead of 1895.

"What the hell are you doing?" Goddess asked. "Your father was born in 1895!"

"What do you care?" I said. "He wanted 1898, we'll give him 1898," I said. And then in Papa's accent I said, "Dat's de vay it's got to be."

So we put 1898 on his gravestone.

Six years later, my mother died and we laid her to rest beside her Sweetheart, and next to David, her firstborn.

Six years after that, we laid Zaki to rest beside the three of them.

A year later, we had the unveiling of Zaki's stone and I looked at the dates on my son's stone and my father's stone and all at once I understood.

We always celebrated Papa's birthday on December Twenty-fourth. But the truth was that neither we nor Papa knew his real birthday. He had been orphaned at eleven and the only thing he knew for sure was that he had been born on Shabbes Hanukah, the first Sabbath of Hanukah.

Papa insisted that we set down in stone the date Shabbes Hanukah 1898.

Zaki left this earth Shabbes Hanukah 1998.

One hundred years to the day.

And Debi had smelled my father on him the night before. And Papa was not just his grandfather but his godfather as well, the one responsible for his spirit and his soul.

So I'll tell you what I believe, and I swear to you these aren't the words of a bereaved father looking to comfort himself.

I believe with a full and complete belief that my father, Zaki's grandfather and godfather, the one responsible for his spirit, was there with him and pulled his soul out so that Zaki would feel no pain, and was there to guide him across, and sent signs to us and messages to let us know that it was so, that there was a plan and Zaki was and is where he is supposed to be, surrounded by those who love him. And that the rabbit and Papa's smell and the dates he insisted be carved in stone and his cousin Greg just happening to be the first paramedic on the scene to take care of Zaki's brothers, that all these things were postcards; postcards from my son that said, got here safe. Don't worry. Love, Zaki.

{ LIFE AFTER LIFE }

I don't believe that Zaki thought his life was nearing its end on this earth, not consciously at any rate. But in the last six months of his sojourn here he simply began to tidy things up. Old friends of his told me later how Zaki had called them out of the blue to say that they hadn't seen each other in too long, or that the last time they had seen each other things had ended badly and Zaki didn't want to leave things that way. He told them how much their friendship meant to him and that he didn't want to leave it on a sour note. Not exactly a twenty-two-year-old type thing to do.

And then there was his thesis film at NYU. It was called *Geometry of Death,* and though meant in part to be a satire on the pretensions of certain French films, it dealt with the inevitability of one particular twenty-two-year-old's death, as certain as a collision course. Not that he was maudlin, because he wasn't in any way. But there was the conversation he'd had with his youngest brother, Adam, in which Adam began offering advice on how Zaki could get his screenplays produced and find the financing for certain indie features Zaki had been trying to get made. Zaki replied in what would heretofore have been a completely uncharacteristic fashion for this young man who had gotten his first feature made at twenty and first book published at nineteen. Zaki told him that it no longer mattered to him if the screenplays were produced or not. He knew how good they were and it was enough for him to know that he had written them.

And then there were our talks in New York that fall, when we were both working on films in his favorite city and meeting at night for dinner, just the two of us. In those talks he told me about what film schools ought to be, as opposed to what they were. Zaki had gone to Columbia for his first two years and loved it because of the classical education it offered. But they would not let undergraduates put their hands on a camera, so he had transferred into NYU for his final two years. He loved living in the Village, where NYU is located, loved the kids there, and loved making his thesis film. But he hated the politics of the school; not politics as in who's going to be president, but school politics, whom you had to suck up to to get your project approved, to get equipment, to get the right production slot, the cliques, the pretenses, and the backstabbing that he saw among some of the students and instructors. And he wanted to do MORE! More films, more scripts, more work! And why did they all have to compartmentalize everything? Beginning camera, beginning sound, directing 101, writing 102, film aesthetics separated from film production and film writing. It made no sense to him. If he could start his own film school, he said, excitement bubbling up over his face, his gestures and voice, there wouldn't be all those separate classes. There would be one class: Movies: Everything You Need to Know. And the thing would be set up in a way to encourage students to help one another rather than look for ways to make themselves look good at another's expense. You could start the thing, he said, on a Monday with showing a great film. You break it down, show why it works directorially and from a writing standpoint, and explain what the tricks in each scene are. Then you assign a scene to the students, get them to try to find the formula or the tricks that made that scene work and then once they think they've figured it out you have them write their own scene about a different subject but using that formula. Then the next day you choose five kids to direct, and everybody crews for them and they shoot their five-minute movies in one week. Then you start all over the next Monday with a different great film. That way it's total immersion. Film criticism would be combined with teaching scene structure, writing would be combined with production and postproduction, and because everyone would be constantly forced to work together because you're cranking out so many films, you would lessen the competition between students and encourage the collaborative nature of it all.

Now why did I go into that long thing about the nature of Zaki's vision of a film school in a book called *Postcards from Heaven?* Good question. Like most of the answers Zaki liked best, this one is a story.

In the spring after Zaki's death, his brothers and mother and I went back to New York. Zaki's thesis film, *Geometry of Death*, was showing in the student film festival. After the screening I met with the woman who was the head of the Tisch School of the Arts. I asked what the largest dollar-amount scholarship was that they had for screenwriting at the film school. She told me that it was, I believe, ten thousand dollars. "Okay," I said. "I'll create a scholarship in the amount of fifteen thousand dollars, to be given each year in perpetuity to the student who writes the best feature-length screenplay." I had a few conditions: that the competition be open both to undergraduates and graduate students and that there be a memorial lecture each year in Zaki's name; I said that I would be happy to give the first one and I would select the winner. The teachers could whittle it down but I wanted to have sole and final say about who received the award. I did this because Zaki was always pissed off about how the students receiving the grants and awards were usually the ones who had sucked up to the right professors as opposed to the ones who were the best writers. Also I felt I was at least as qualified as any of their teaching staff to make that judgment. I have ten produced features on which I am credited by the Writers Guild of America, as well as several hundred hours of television, five published novels, and four produced plays. I would not have asked to choose the most promising mathematician or nuclear physicist, but I do know a bit about writing.

102 / Postcards *from* Heaven

The woman who was head of the school answered, basically, Here's the way it works. "You give us money, we decide how to spend it." I walked out the door, took a cab uptown to Columbia University, and divided the fifteen thousand dollars into three awards, which are now given at Columbia University, UCLA, and USC as the Zaki Gordon Awards for Excellence in Screenwriting. They are open to undergraduates and graduates alike and there is a memorial lecture at each school every year, and each year I look forward to reading the scripts that are submitted. But that's not the story. Here's the story:

That summer I was flying up to Calgary for the wedding of one of my cousins, one of Uncle Hyman's grandsons. I was sitting next to a woman and we began to talk.

"Why are you going to Calgary?"

"My cousin's wedding. Why are you going to Calgary?" I asked her. She was going to look at a cultural park.

"What's a cultural park?" I asked.

"We have one in Sedona, Arizona," she said. "It's a large, beautiful tract of land overlooking the red rocks and there's an amphitheater on it and we have a building that was going to be a museum but now we're going to use it to house a film school."

"What kind of film school?" I asked.

"That's just the problem," she said. "We have no idea what kind of film school. They were going to use the building for a museum but when that fell through the local community college said they wanted it and the county supervisors said okay, but you've got to put something in there that we don't already have. Well, they said, how about a film school? The supervisors said fine. But the truth is we don't have any idea about what kind of film school to put in or why anyone would want to come to our film school instead of someone else's."

"I'll tell you why they'd want to come there," I said.

"Why?" she asked.

"Because it's going to be the best hands-on program in the world, unlike any other film school there is, and the classes aren't going to be divided up into, you know, beginning directing, beginning sound, film aesthetics 101 . . ." and I began pitching her Zaki's vision for what a film school ought to be.

Three weeks later I was in Sedona, Arizona. It took six months of negotiations between the community college and the nonprofit corporation I had set up, but today The Zaki Gordon Institute for Independent Filmmaking is in its eighth year. Several hundred students have already graduated. We have made roughly 1,000 five-minute films, 250 thirty-minute thesis films, and three feature-length films. We have added a documentary track as well as our narrative program to train filmmakers in that discipline. Last year, after only seven years in existence, two students from The Zaki Gordon Institute for Independent Filmmaking were named as finalists in the Student Academy Awards, which is to say that two Zaki students were honored as being among the top fifty student filmmakers in the country. Two students out of a school with an enrollment of forty. Three years ago we were one of six film schools in the country to receive a special grant from Kodak to set up a second-year professional program for selected students. We are a member of CILECT, the International Society of Film and Television Schools, and our students' films have appeared in festivals around the world.

Because we are part of a community college we are open to anyone eighteen years of age and up regardless of academic background. Also because we are part of a community college, our students range from eighteen-year-old kids to seventy-plus-year-old kids, with equal numbers of people in their sixties, fifties, forties, and thirties. We have had students from England, Ireland, Thailand, Japan, Spain, Australia, Tonga, Egypt, and Brazil. They come in every color—red, brown, black, yellow, and off-white—and every religion including Hopi, Navajo, Islam, Jade, and Hindi. We have Born Agains and Buddhist nuns. Being in northern Arizona, we're a little short on Jews.

Just before the school was set to open, the guy who was going to be director, a wonderful man who had been Zaki's film instructor in high school and is one of the premier film educators in the country, Russell Cooper-Mead, had a heart attack. His doctor wouldn't allow him to accept the post. Another guy, an old friend who was retiring from his teaching position at UCLA, said yes and then decided to stay at UCLA for another few years. We were only weeks away from opening and didn't have a director. I would be teaching one day a week, showing the classic film and breaking it down for students, but we needed a director of the school not only as an administrator but to teach camera. We would hold seminars on the weekends with professionals from Hollywood flying in and volunteering their time, but no director meant no school. My then assistant, Ms. Crystal Jordan, to whom I will forever be in debt, suggested a friend of hers, just to fill in until we got someone permanent, Stephan Schultze, a director of photography. He was between films. I begged him to fill in just for three to six months, just till . . .

Steph is now in his eighth year and has made the program his own. It is his life's work and the school will be his legacy. He has created a school that can compete on an international level with the best in the world. Under Steph's direction, the school is now a cosponsor of the Sedona International Film Festival and administers the Zaki Gordon Awards, making us the only film school in the world that grants scholarships to other film schools as well as its own. Steph met his wife, Lori, because of the school and she is now one of the school's administrators. Students have gotten married and babies have been born because of the school.

One of the hallmarks of Zaki students is how wonderfully supportive they are of one another, how nurturing of one another's talents and proud of one another's accomplishments. Each year the school hosts the Zaki Awards and we fly out the winners from Columbia University, UCLA, USC, and Viewpoint School, Zaki's old high school. In addition, we have granted scholarships at the Sam Spiegel Film and Television School in Jerusalem and Tel Aviv University.

All of it stems from Zaki's philosophy and vision, which he outlined in program notes of his feature film, *Waiting for Mo*. It is our school's manifesto:

> *People my age are visually literate without film school. We cut our teeth on videos made in high school and see no separation between folks who make the stuff you see on screen and the people who watch it. We turn to do-it-yourself filmmaking, not after years of frustration in the Biz, but right away. Because it is a valid way to make films. Because you can make a good film in your hometown with your friends, your savings. Soon someone will pop out of every town in America with a small film made on a shoestring budget, telling their story the best they can. Some will make fresh brilliant films and some will make utter crap. But if you want to find the next wave of filmmakers you don't need to look at those working their way up the ladder in Hollywood or even those making shorts at USC, UCLA or NYU. Maybe look at the kid on the corner with the video camera. We are proud that "Waiting for Mo" is one of the early films of the next wave. We are proud that we made a little film about kids hanging out in the Valley with lives just like ours, just like a lot of kids in a lot of towns with stories to tell.*

At the Zaki Gordon Memorial Lecture at USC, a young girl came up to me after the lecture and said that she had known Zaki at NYU. She was drop-dead gorgeous, and I thought, *I bet you and Zaki knew each other.* Zaki would not have let her go unnoticed. She told me how they had shared a directing class. She had pitched an idea for a film and everyone jumped on it. It was too bourgeois, they had said, too this and much too that. Zaki was the only one who had stood up and said, "Don't listen to them, because if that's your story, that's the one you've got to tell." It sounded like Zaki, and not just like Zaki coming on to a beautiful girl.

Two years later, one of our graduating students came up to me after commencement exercises. She said she wanted to tell me something. She said she'd had a dream about Zaki. Well, I found that sort of off-putting in an odd way. Perhaps it was my mood. Commencement at Zaki is a bittersweet thing for me. Besides, how could she dream of Zaki? There are purposely no pictures of Zaki up at the school. The reason is that I never wanted the place to be a memorial to him, never wanted it to just be his name on the wall. Rather, the place is meant to be a living entity, full of the excitement of artistic creation and the unique joy of friendship with kindred spirits. So how could she have dreamed of Zaki? Instead of saying any of this, I just said, "Oh . . . well, that's nice."

She felt compelled to tell me her dream. She was trying to decide whether to do a certain project or not. She wanted to do it but was afraid that people wouldn't accept it or even find it interesting.

"That's when I heard this voice, and I don't know why but I knew it was Zaki, and he said to me, 'Listen, if that's your story, that's the one you've got to tell.'"

I fought back tears and said, well, I guess you did dream of Zaki. She made the film. It was bought by PBS.

The cofounder of the Zaki Gordon Institute for Independent Filmmaking is Dr. Doreen Dailey, the former president of Yavapai College. She fought long and hard to get and protect our budget and at the same time ensure the uniqueness of our program, which would have been bureaucratted to death at any other institution. One day, for seemingly no reason, she asked, "Have you ever wondered why I was such a proponent of this school?"

"Because you thought it was a good idea?"

"There are a lot of good ideas."

"Why then?" I asked.

Doreen told me that she had had a rough childhood, one full of many challenges that in a lesser person would never have been overcome. She said she owed everything to a man who became her mentor. When she was going to drop out of school he pushed her to achieve academic excellence, to get first her BA and then her master's degree and finally her doctorate. She said she would have been nothing without his guidance and love.

Nice story, I thought, *but what's that got to do with our school?*

His name, she said, was Zack Gordon.

Try to calculate the odds against the utter perfection of that design and you will go insane.

Zaki has come to me several times in dreams, though I don't really know if they were dreams. It is about two o'clock in the morning. I know I am asleep, and then I hear his voice. Not as if in a dream, but right there next to me.

One occurred when I was writing the stage adaptation of the motion picture *Terms of Endearment*. It is a story that deals, ultimately, with the death of an adult child. I was having a tough time with the last scene. If you recall the movie, which starred Shirley MacLaine and Jack Nicholson, you will remember that the last scene is a kind of wake that takes place in the mother's backyard. The husband and children of Emma, the young woman who has passed away, are there, as are the mother's former suitors.

There was no way that I could re-create that onstage. For reasons of economics, which dictate that five or six characters are the most you can have in a non musical play today, I had cut out Emma's husband and children as well as the mother's former suitors. You hear about all of them in conversations between mother and daughter but you never see them onstage. Thus, the final scene could not be re-created since I had written most of the characters out of the play. There I was with a play that did not have a climactic scene, one that would sum up all the emotion of the drama and, I hoped, provide a kind of healing resolution. I had a play without an ending. And I didn't have a clue as to how to go about finding one.

That's when I heard Zaki's voice at two o'clock in the morning, right there, right next to me in the dark, saying, "Schmuck, just call me. That's all you have to do."

I was fully awake then and I knew exactly how to end the play. Like most parents with grown children in today's world, the majority of my conversations with Zaki after he left home were over the phone. He lived in New York. I lived in L.A. Yoni today is a musician living in Boston and Adam is a college basketball coach in Florida. We're on the phone a lot. After the accident I found myself many times unconsciously dialing Zaki's number to tell him this or that. It was only when I would hear his answering-machine greeting that I remembered . . . and then I would stay on the line just to hear his voice once again.

So now at two o'clock in the morning, having heard his voice right there, right next to me in the dark, I got up and, with moon-light streaming through the window, I handwrote the last scene of the play, per Zaki's instruction.

(Aurora enters wearing a black coat having just returned from a memorial service. She paces ner-vously, still wiping away tears, a stranger in her own home. She sits, she stands, and finally she crosses to the phone and dials, almost as if not realizing whom she is calling. The phone rings three times. And

then we hear the sound of an answering machine,
and Emma's sweet voice on the recording.)

EMMA (on recording)

Hello, you've reached the Horton family. This is Emma.
We're not around to take your call but if you leave a message at the beep, we'll get back as soon as we can. Have a
great day.

(Aurora stands there, her daughter's voice still
hanging in the air.)

AURORA

Hi, sweetheart. It's mom . . . I just came back from your
memorial service and I needed to call someone, so I dialed
your number without realizing it . . . because you're the
one I always called. It was a beautiful service; we played
the song you asked for.

(Softly in the background we begin to hear the
recording of "I'll Be Seeing You," which plays
under Aurora's dialogue.)

AURORA

Poor Flap. He couldn't stop crying. I think he never realized until now how much he really loved you. Little Mel-
anie has the astronaut wrapped around her finger. He's
already made plans to pay for her ballet lessons. Leave it
to him to wind up with a pretty young girl, but the truth is
she might be too old for him. Tommy and Teddy were just
sitting on the steps and I went over and sat down between
them, but they were both still sitting so far away and there
was so much I wanted to say to them. But all I could do
was motion with my hand and say come a little closer . . . a
little closer . . . a little closer . . . a little closer.

(She lowers the phone to her heart as the music swells and she crosses up to the bedroom window, her face bathed in moonlight as the final lyrics of the song "I'll Be Seeing You" are heard.)

SONG

I'll be looking at the moon . . .

But I'll be seeing you.

(The curtain falls.)

Postcards . . . They're not profound, not weighty tomes on the nature of the universe. Usually they're nothing more than a pretty picture of a faraway place with a sweet message:

Got here safe.

It's really beautiful.

Much love till we meet again.

Dan Gordon

Shabbes Hanukah 2007

{ Note to Reader }

Thank you for taking the time to read *Postcards from Heaven*.
If these stories have touched you, please let me know. Also, if
you have received "postcards" of your own and would like to
share them with me and others, please contact me at my Web
site, www.postcardsfromheavenonline.com.

{ Acknowledgments }

Though the writing of this book was cathartic, it was, as well, an emotional ride. It was written originally for members of my own family, and to them goes my heartfelt thanks for reading the manuscript as well as for their love and support. In particular, to my cousins, Donna, Manuel, Betty, Deborah, Jo-Ann, and Jennifer, and my niece Danielle. To my sons Yoni and Adam, as always, my appreciation for being the best sounding boards, the best friends, and the best sons any father could ever ask for. Nachas. It's a word we've discussed, and now you know what it means. To Linda Gray, who is as wise as she is beautiful, and who among other things is my rabbi, and teacher. To Donna Loffredo and Leslie Meredith at Free Press and to my agent Ryan Fischer-Harbage, my thanks for your support of this book and of me, which was unwavering and always deeply, deeply appreciated. To Joel Gotler for passing this on and recommending me to Ryan. To Matt O'Neill, my able assistant, my gratitude for all your hard work.

Once again I much appreciate the reader taking the time to live these pages with me.

{ ABOUT THE AUTHOR }

Dan Gordon was born in California and educated both there and in Israel. He is the screenwriter of such motion pictures as *The Hurricane*, which starred Denzel Washington; *Wyatt Earp*, with Kevin Costner; *Murder in the First*, with Kevin Bacon and Christian Slater; *The Assignment*, with Sir Ben Kingsley, Aidan Quinn, and Donald Sutherland; and is the co-screenwriter of *The Celestine Prophecy*. His stage adaptations include *Terms of Endearment*, which starred Linda Gray in the U.K. production, and *Rain Man* which will have made its West End of London debut in the summer of 2008, starring Josh Hartnett; as well as *Irena's Vow* starring Tovah Feldshuh, set for a fall 2008 off-Broadway production. In addition, he is the co-founder of the Zaki Gordon Institute for Independent Filmmaking in Sedona, Arizona.

Portions from the proceeds of this book will go to benefit the Zaki Gordon Memorial Charitable Gift Fund and the Zaki Gordon Institute for Independent Filmmaking.